A Brief History of
Saints

D0616642

Blackwell Brief Histories of
Religion

This series offers brief, accessible, and lively accounts of key topics within theology and religion. Each volume presents both academic and general readers with a selected history of topics which have had a profound effect on religious and cultural life. The word "history" is, therefore, understood in its broadest cultural and social sense. The volumes are based on serious scholarship but they are written engagingly and in terms readily understood by general readers.

Published

Alister E. McGrath – A Brief History of Heaven
G. R. Evans – A Brief History of Heresy
Tamara Sonn – A Brief History of Islam
Douglas J. Davies – A Brief History of Death
Lawrence S. Cunningham – A Brief History of Saints

Forthcoming

Michael Banner – A Brief History of Ethics
Carter Lindberg – A Brief History of Love
Carter Lindberg – A Brief History of Christianity
Dana Robert – A Brief History of Mission
Philip Sheldrake – A Brief History of Spirituality
Kenneth Appold – A Brief History of the Reformation
Dennis D. Martin – A Brief History of Monasticism
Martha Himmelfarb – A Brief History of the Apocalypse

A Brief History of
Saints

LAWRENCE S. CUNNINGHAM

Blackwell
Publishing

© 2005 by Lawrence S. Cunningham

BLACKWELL PUBLISHING
350 Main Street, Malden, MA 02148-5020, USA
108 Cowley Road, Oxford OX4 1JF, UK
550 Swanston Street, Carlton, Victoria 3053, Australia

First published 2005 by Blackwell Publishing Ltd

Library of Congress Cataloging-in-Publication Data
Cunningham, Lawrence.
  A brief history of saints / Lawrence S. Cunningham.
    p. cm.—(Blackwell brief histories of religion)
  Includes bibliographical references and index.
  ISBN 1-4051-1401-0 (hardcover : alk. paper)—ISBN 1-4051-1402-9
(pbk : alk. paper) 1. Christian saints—Cult—History. 2.
Canonization—History. I. Title. II. Series.

BX2333.C86 2004
235′.2′09—dc22

                                                    2004011685

A catalogue record for this title is available from the British Library.

Set in 10/12.5pt Meridien
by Graphicraft Limited, Hong Kong
Printed and bound in the United Kingdom
by TJ International, Padstow, Cornwall

The publisher's policy is to use permanent paper from mills that operate a sustainable forestry policy, and which has been manufactured from pulp processed using acid-free and elementary chlorine-free practices. Furthermore, the publisher ensures that the text paper and cover board used have met acceptable environmental accreditation standards.

For further information on
Blackwell Publishing, visit our website:
www.blackwellpublishing.com

Contents

Illustrations

Introduction

The popular American singer, Billy Joel, sings a lyric in which he confesses that he would rather "laugh with the sinner / than cry with the saints." By contrast, the old New Orleans jazz favorite "When the Saints Go Marching in" insists that "I want to be among that number . . ." These two popular songs indicate the two polar images of saints: on the one hand, dreary, pinched, and lugubrious mourners and haters of a good time and, on the other, the glorious end of human life.

The matter of the saints is not made easier because we are the heirs of a long artistic tradition, most amply documented in old Roman Catholic churches, of figures who seem to have lived in a distant past and whose background is almost always depicted in gold leaf. Many Catholics of a certain age have had their image of saints shaped profoundly by holy cards, stained-glass windows, garishly polychromed plaster-of-Paris statues, as well as innumerable paintings that are often jejeune and sentimental. Some of this older art is valued as works of high culture, while a good deal of it found in local parishes is luridly bad. Some saints are identified with ethnic pride. In the city where I reside, the churches founded by immigrant communities in the late nineteenth and early twentieth centuries tell an informed person where the communities originated because the newcomers brought their patronal saints with them: Saint Patrick (Ireland), Saint Bavo (Belgium), Saint Adalbert (Poland), Saint Stephen (Hungary), Saint Antony of Padua (Italy), and so on.

It is also true that some saints have found admirers because they have been sentimentalized to fit the age. Every self-respecting suburban garden center can supply a concrete statue of Saint Francis with a bird perched on his shoulder, and over thirty filmmakers, going back before the "talkies," have given us versions of Saint Joan of Arc. Other saints, like Valentine (there were actually two martyrs of that name), have become submerged into the popular sentimentality of the greeting-card companies and chocolate manufacturers. Chicago's Saint Patrick's Day includes turning the city's river green with vegetable dye. The mutation of the Eastern Saint Nicholas of Myra into Santa Claus will be narrated in its proper place. One must decide whether the sentimentality of the religious person or that of the secular one is the more misleading.

This brief history of saints will focus on the roots, development, and significance of the saints in the Christian tradition in general and in the Roman Catholic tradition more particularly. My decision to emphasize the Roman Catholic Church in this work derives from a twofold conviction. First, one should speak only about those things about which one knows something. As a Roman Catholic teaching in a Catholic university, one of my research interests has been the meaning and significance of the saints, but in the course of my work I have kept my eye on the tradition of the saints in other Christian communities and that interest will be honored in this work. Second, most readers in the West are more familiar with the Roman Catholic tradition of the saints if for no other reason than that most of our major museums well represent that tradition, and, further, that our popular culture still has lingering memories of the old tradition of the cult of the saints, even if most people could not say who the aforementioned Saint Valentine was or how Saint Nicholas became Santa Claus. We will pay a fair amount of attention to the Christian East because Orthodoxy does share a robust cult of the saints, even though many who do not belong to that ancient Christian tradition are unfamiliar with it.

There will be more than one occasion in this work when the argument will be made that the tradition of the saints should be of interest to others besides social historians, students of iconography, folklorists, and experts in popular religion. In fact, given the current rise in serious concerns about the nature and practice of Christian spirituality, the lives of the saints, both ancient and contemporary, provide a precious resource for that interest. The tradition of the saints is, in fact, an under-used resource for theological reflection. Moreover, as the final chapter will suggest, the tradition of the "Friends of God" is a possible launching point for serious inter-religious dialogue. After all, as Pope John Paul II observed in his encyclical letter *Ut Unum Sint* (1995), authentic dialogue should begin as an "exchange of gifts." One great gift that Christianity possesses is the unbroken witness of heroic figures, both men and women, who have exemplified this or that aspect of the Christian life. Other traditions have their own exemplary figures to tell us about.

We shall also see that the subject of saints in the long tradition of Christianity is a complex one. Many saints are known to us only by name to which fantastic folktales have become appended with imagination supplying what history lacks. Other saints strike us as odd, outrageous, or eccentric. The late medieval mystic Richard Rolle was so peculiar that his sister cried out: *Frater meus insanus est* (My brother is bonkers). Still others were luminous in their person to an extent that even today they have an allure for the contemporary seeker. Very early in this work we will have to spend some energy trying to figure out a usable description of what it is that we are talking about. This will not be an easy task as will soon become patent.

This brief work has six chapters that follow an historical trajectory from the beginnings of the Christian story down to the present. Of necessity, it tells that story at a rather brisk pace. The enormous amount of both primary and secondary literature on the saints necessitates picking and choosing. An incomplete bibliography of literature on the saints, published two decades ago in Stephen Wilson's *Saints and their Cults* (1983), had over thirteen hundred items in it. Cascades of studies continue to appear each year and from angles that are quite diverse. The modest bibliography at the end of this book includes three bibliographical essays done by myself which indicate a partial list of works, mainly books, that came to my attention in the 1990s. The Select Bibliography includes a number of resources for the study of saints. With some very important exceptions, I have limited that bibliography to items in the English language.

The vast body of secondary literature on the saints, almost impossible to be mastered by a single person, necessitated a certain selectivity not only about what is touched on in this short book but how it should be treated. Nobody could be more conscious than I am of how quickly this book slides over vexatious issues or generalizes where more nuance might have been expected. Readers must see this work as only a first word, while I live in hope that it spurs further reading and reflection.

A number of people have assisted me in finishing this project. I am in debt to the chair of the Department of Theology, Professor John Cavadini, for creating such a wonderful academic community within which to work. Reverend Professor Richard McBrien, himself a student of the saints, has been generous with his time and his knowledge, as has Reverend Professor Maxwell Johnson whose assistance with matters liturgical, including the use of some of his books, has been a great help. The editorial staff of Blackwell Publishing have been most supportive. I would like to give particular thanks to Rebecca Harkin, who recruited me for this task, and Sophie Gibson, who saw it through to its finish.

This little book, as always, is for the three women in my life: my wife Cecilia and my daughters Sarah Mary and Julia Clare.

Chapter 1

The Saint: Beginnings

A Saint is a peculiar being.

John Henry Newman

Alban Butler (1711–73), descended from a distinguished recusant family from Northhamptonshire, was sent by his family to the English College at Douai on the continent where he became, in time, one of its professors. Ordained a Roman Catholic priest in 1735, he labored, mainly on the continent, but with occasional visits back to England, for thirty years to complete research in order to write his *The Lives of the Saints*, which was published in London in four huge octavo volumes between 1756 and 1759. Subsequent editions in the eighteenth and nineteenth centuries appeared in Dublin and Edinburgh. *The Lives of the Saints* is part of that central library of recusant literature associated with Douai in France, which takes its place with such works as the Douai–Rheims translation of the Bible from the Latin Vulgate (the Roman Catholic alternative to the Authorized Version) and the very popular manual of prayers known as *The Garden of the Soul*. These three works – *The Lives of the Saints*, the Douai–Rheims Bible, and the prayer book – were staples of Roman Catholic life in English-speaking countries well into the twentieth century. My father used a copy of *The Garden of the Soul* (inherited from his father) for his devotions well into the 1960s.

In the twentieth century, there were augmentations and corrections to the original volumes of Butler's *Lives* under various editors, first in 1928 by Herbert Thurston, SJ, and in the 1950s by the same editor and the late Donald Attwater. The last edition in twelve volumes (one for each month of the year) was published in the 1990s under the general editorship of Paul Burns.[1] The work as a whole, edited and updated as it has been, has never gone out of print, even though it has only been this final edition that has appeared in twelve volumes. It will require further updating soon given the pace of canonizations and beatifications under the pontificate of John Paul II.

Butler's *Lives* is organized according to the months of the year. Each day records the saints of the Catholic Church who are venerated either universally in the Roman calendar or locally in a specific geographical area or within a particular religious order. The entries in Butler try to reflect all of the saints who appear in the authoritative Roman martyrology,[2] although it cannot take into account all the saints beatified or canonized by Pope John Paul II since 1995.

One can open any of the volumes of Butler's *Lives* to any day to see immediately why we can speak of the saints as a "problem" in the sense that one finds it hard, frequently, to know what the persons listed for a given day have in common. The entries for May 30 are not atypical. We commemorate on that day the feast of Saints Basil and Emmelia, whose claim to fame is that they were the parents of four great fourth-century Cappadocian figures: Saints Gregory of Nyssa, Peter of Sebastea, Basil the Great, and Macrina the Younger. The same day also commemorates the seventh-century martyr Saint Dympna about whom we know nothing; what is told of her in the hagiographical tradition, is, in fact, all derived from folktales. Further, we also note an entry on Saint Hubert, who is alleged to be the founder of the town of Liège in Belgium but whose body is now in the French Ardennes city of St Hubert. He is the patron of hunters (because his life story was confused with that of Saint Eustace – the conflation of the lives of the saints is not uncommon) and, for unclear reasons, he is traditionally invoked against hydrophobia or rabies. We also honor, on the same day, a Spanish king, Ferdinand of Castile and a little-known English saint from Norfolk named Walstan. Better known, however, is Saint Joan of Arc who was executed for heresy, later rehabilitated, and finally canonized. Her story has so caught the popular imagination that over thirty films have been made of her life dating back to the era of silent movies. She has also been honored by dramatic plays (for example by George Bernard Shaw) and any number of works in sculpture and painting. Joan's life also illustrates the complexity of being named a saint. She was executed as a relapsed heretic on May 30, 1431. In 1456, Pope Callistus III declared that the process that had condemned her had been unjust, but it was not until 1920 that she was canonized in the papacy of Pope Benedict XV.

If, then, one came innocently to those entries in Butler's *Lives* for May 30 it would be reasonable to ask if we were speaking of a single category of person. What could possibly be the link that ties together a medieval Spanish king, a fourth-century husband and wife, semi-legendary figures like Dympna, who is now associated with help for those suffering mental illness, and a fifteenth-century cross-dressing adolescent who heard heavenly voices (of saints who may or may not have existed in fact) which provoked her to lead an army? The short answer to the question is not much beyond the fact that they are all listed as saints in the Roman martyrology. Indeed, if one is to make any sense out of the category of "saint" as it is traditionally understood in the historic Christian church, or, at a minimum, begin to understand if this heterogeneous collection of edifying tales and moral exempla even add up to what Wittgenstein, in an inspired phrase, calls a "family resemblance," we need to sort out what is, in fact, a very complex and trying story. This first chapter will attempt to set the stage for this extremely convoluted tale.

Beginnings

The word "saint" is part of the common coinage of our language. We say that someone would "try the patience of a saint" or that one's mother was a saint. In general, the word "saint" in the common vernacular has connotations of forbearance, self-abnegation, and service to others out of love. At a second level, we might also think of church names, figures cast in plaster-of-Paris, pictures in museums of maidens being fed to lions, medallions on chains worn about the neck depicting Saint Christopher, certain holidays like Saint Patrick's Day, and other ephemera derived from popular Catholicism. Among those Christians who venerate the saints there is also the strong conviction that they can be instructive in attempts to live the Christian life. We learn of love for the natural world from a Saint Francis or bravery in facing a hostile, unbelieving world from the martyrs or how to pray better from spiritual masters and mistresses like the great mystics. Functionally speaking, the saints serve a variety of purposes in the historic Christian church, but taken as a whole they represent a very complex phenomenon.

It is at this second level of discourse that we find the subject of our study. We want to know how these various kinds of saints came to be, what they mean, and how they fit into the larger discourse of Christianity in general (for example, what does the creed mean by the "communion of saints"?) and Catholic Christianity (broadly understood) in particular. To answer such questions, we need both to look back into history and, at another level, to reflect critically. This work, then, has two strains within it: history and theological reflection.

We do find the word "saint" in the vernacular versions of Christian Scriptures. Saint Paul frequently uses the Greek word *agios* as a generic term for members of the early Christian communities. He greets the community at Rome who are "called to be saints" (Rom. 1: 7). He uses a similar phrase in his greeting to the church at Corinth (1 Cor. 1: 2) and, in his second letter, he salutes that church again, adding "all the saints throughout Achaia" (2 Cor. 1: 1). He addresses the "saints who are in Ephesus" (Eph. 1: 1), and further on tells the Gentile members that they are no longer strangers and aliens but "citizens with the saints and members of the household of God" (Eph. 2: 19). To the church at Philippi he expands his greeting: "to all the saints in Christ Jesus who are in Philippi" (Phil. 1: 1). A variation of that expanded greeting can be found in Paul's letter to Colossae: "To the saints and brothers and sisters in Christ in Colossae" (Col. 1: 2).

What does Paul mean by this terminology? It seems clear that Paul understands the members of the community to be holy and, in this generic sense, saints. Another way of describing a saint would be, in this sense, to describe a "holy person." The biblical tradition posits holiness essentially as a characteristic of God. God is holy. Everything else – people, places, things, actions, rites, buildings, books, and so on – become holy to the degree that they are linked to or identified with the holiness of God. When Paul speaks of the "holy ones" (i.e. the saints) of the early Christian communities, he means to say that by their identification with God, through the saving works of Christ, they have become linked to and identified with God and, in this sense, are saints. Holiness, then, is ascribable to a person to the degree that he or she is somehow connected to the source of holiness, which is God. The first letter of Peter makes the point explicitly: "Instead, as he [i.e. Jesus Christ] who called you is holy, be holy yourselves in all your conduct, for it is written, 'You shall be holy, for I am holy'" (1 Pet. 1: 15–16, quoting Lev. 11: 44–5). In the New Testament, finally, the "saint" is one who merits the name even during life. The "saint" is close to God and those who are not saints (the impious) are not close to God.

This general understanding of "saint" or "holy one" has remained within the Christian community down to the present day. We describe the community as a "communion of saints" and describe the church as holy in the sense that Christians, singly and in community, are called to be close to God in Christ. The dogmatic constitution on the church (*Lumen Gentium*), promulgated at the Second Vatican Council of the Roman Catholic Church, asserted that there is a universal call to holiness for everyone irrespective of their state of life.[3] It goes on to say that the clearest proof of this holiness in the Christian community "is brilliantly proved by the lives of so many saints in church history" (*Lumen Gentium* no. 40). Not to put too fine a point on it: all are called to be saints, but in the history of the Christian tradition some people are distinguished by their holiness and those people are the "saints" in the more restrictive sense. It is to that category of person that this study addresses itself.

We should further stipulate that the place of saints is a conspicuous part of Roman Catholic, Orthodox, Anglican, and Lutheran life, while other church bodies with roots in the sixteenth-century Reformation either ignore or militate against any special class of persons who are called "saints" in the restrictive sense in which we will use the term. How these distinctions came into play will be discussed in their proper place in subsequent chapters of this book. This short history of the saints will deal, then, with both the maintenance of the saintly tradition and its sloughing off in certain forms of Christianity.

The Second Vatican Council's dogmatic constitution on the church (*Lumen Gentium*) gives us a clue about how this publicly and liturgically recognized category of saints emerged in the Christian church. After glossing the various paths of Christian holiness, *Lumen Gentium* goes on to say: "From the earliest times, then, some Christians have been called upon – and some will always be called upon – to give this supreme testimony of love for all people, but especially to persecutors. The church, therefore, considers martyrdom as an exceptional gift and as the highest proof of love" (no. 42). The phrase "from earliest times" indicates a path mark for us because it is in the experience of the early Christian martyrs that the whole history of devotion to the saints, and their place in the Christian experience, begins.

The Martyrs

It is an incontestable fact that the early Christian movement suffered persecution at the hands of the authorities of the Roman empire, which continued in fits and starts within the generation after the earthly life of Jesus and continued down until the early fourth century.[4] Tradition has it that there were ten periods of persecution, but that may be a pious fiction in order to have the Christian persecutions somehow mirror the ten plagues of the Old Testament. The periods of persecution and their intensity were episodic, flaring up in this or that particular place in the empire. Roman writers attest to such persecutions. Tacitus, writing in the *Annales* early in the second century, describes the Christians – for whom he held no love – as becoming scapegoats for the burning of the city during the reign of Nero. They were worried to death by wild dogs or set alight as living flambeaus in Nero's circus. Early in the second century, Pliny the Younger wrote to the emperor from near the Black Sea, describing his handling of Christians found in his area of jurisdiction: if they did not worship the genius of the emperor, he had them executed.

It was only in the middle of the third century, in the year 250 during the reign of the emperor Decius, that there was an empire-wide persecution of Christians, triggered by a decree that in that year all persons were to honor the Roman gods by public acts of homage in a temple and by obtaining a certificate to that effect. In the latter half of the third century and early in the fourth century, under the emperors Valerian and Diocletian, there were similar widespread acts against the Christians. These large persecutions came after nearly two centuries of anti-Christian legislation and punishment in various parts of the empire. The best evidence is that, apart from these widespread campaigns, the persecutions of Christians were episodic, local or regional, albeit, at times, ferocious.

What caused the Christians to be the subject of Roman persecution? The issue is not all that clear. What is clear is that just being a "Christian" from the time of Nero was sufficient cause for state intervention. It is most likely that the Romans saw the Christians as undermining the civic virtue of *pietas*: that mixture of love and fear that ideally reigned in the Roman family as children showed *pietas* to their parents, which the family, in turn, showed to the state, and the state manifested to the gods. The Christian refusal to render such *pietas* to the gods seemed, from the Roman point of view, to be an act of treason: a fifth column of dissidents who eroded the *pax deorum*, that peace of the gods which alone guaranteed the stability and flourishing of the Roman state. In short, despite the efforts of second-century Christian writers like the apologist Justin (who himself died in Rome as a martyr in 165 AD), who argued that Christians could be good citizens despite their abstinence from Roman religious rites, the Christians were seen as a dangerous sect at odds with the commonweal.

Looked at from the vantage point of the success of Christianity in the West, it is difficult for people nowadays to grasp that early Christianity was a counter-cultural force at odds with the regnant sentiments of their contemporaries. The Christians became easy targets for popular discontent. As the powerful third-century rhetorical writer in North Africa, Tertullian, put it: "If the Tiber has overflowed its banks, if the Nile has remained in its bed, if the sky has been still, or the earth been in commotion, if death has made its devastations, or famine its afflictions, your cry immediately is 'Christians to the lions!'" (*Apology* no. 40). Tertullian knew of what he spoke since his native city of Carthage in North Africa had long experience of Christian persecution.

It was only in the early fourth century, with the Edict of Toleration issued by the emperor Constantine in Milan, that the age of the martyrs came to a close. By that time the role of the martyrs had already taken a cultural and theological contour that would contribute to the future shape of the Christian understanding of saints and their significance in the larger Christian theological and devotional life. A number of factors contributed to that understanding.

Literature

First, an enormous literature, developed by the Christian community in response to Roman persecution, began to take shape quite early. That literature took various forms. The second-century apologists addressed the Roman public with at least two lines of argument to counter the official persecution of the Christians by government intervention: that what the Christians believed (despite scurrilous rumors about sexual orgies, secret plotting, and even cannibalism) was not immoral or poisonous to the common good and, further, that the Christian unwillingness to honor the Roman deities did not a priori mean that they were bad citizens or, worse, subversive enemies of the Roman state. Some of that literature had a polemical edge to it as these early writers not only argued for the benign character of Christian teaching but, in the process, advanced the idea that pagan religion was grossly deficient and pagan philosophy at best a preparation for the Gospel or that the best of pagan thought actually derived from the Bible. The most well known of these apologies, written by the second-century Justin Martyr, exemplifies this approach. That he bears the title "martyr" indicates that he was not all that persuasive since he was executed as a Christian in Rome around the year 165.

A quite different kind of literature also grew up in the second century. This literature was a kind of memory bank produced by early Christian communities to keep the recollection of those who suffered alive.[5] The earliest strata of that literature are the so-called *Acta* of the judicial processes by which the Christians were tried and condemned. We possess, for example, the main part of the process which condemned Justin Martyr and six other Christians. The text consists of a brief interrogation which determined that the seven were Christians and would not sacrifice to the gods. The sentence was brief and to the point: "Let those who will not sacrifice to the gods and yield to the command of the emperor [i.e. Marcus Aurelius the famous Stoic] be scourged and led away to be beheaded in accordance with the law."

A second, more full kind of literature is known as the *Passio* or the *Martyrium*. These are elaborated texts that describe the sufferings of the martyr(s) in some detail; often one finds an echo of the *Acta* embedded within these texts. What makes these *Passiones* of considerable interest is that they were written by one church community for the sake of another to provide an account of a martyr's death; that is, they were a kind of encyclical letter meant to be read aloud in Christian communities. As a consequence, these documents give us some insight into what the early community thought about the significance of those who witnessed unto death. Several of these texts have taken on classic status in early Christian literature. *The Passion of Perpetua and Felicity*, for example, is a third-century text (compiled by Tertullian himself?) which, in part, is autobiographical, which means that it is, at least in part, the earliest known Christian text written by a woman – the Perpetua of the title. The full text describes the condemnation of a young noble woman, Perpetua, and her servant, Felicity, as well as some others who were exposed to the wild beasts in the circus of Carthage. The text, with its dream sequences and theological reflections, has received intense interest from scholars. The one thing that is very clear is that both Perpetua and Felicity were central to the story and cast in an heroic mold.

Of particular interest for our purposes is the second-century text known as *The Martyrdom of Polycarp*, written by the church community at Smyrna to the church at Philomelium to describe "those who suffered martyrdom, especially the blessed Polycarp." The text is a narrative of the events leading up to the death of the aged bishop, but what is more interesting is the theological framework within which the story is told. The writer puts it succinctly: "Almost everything that led up to it happened in order that the Lord might show once again a martyrdom conformable to the Gospel." In other words, the martyr performed, as it were, an end to life similar to the supreme martyr of the Christian faith, Jesus, who died on the cross under a sentence also pronounced by the Roman authorities. The text is written in such a fashion that it is studded with narrative parallels to the passion of Christ. Hence, the martyr's death was seen against the template of the passion of Christ who provides the template for giving up one's life.

This insistence on the martyr's imitation of Christ is close to another second-century text, the *Letter of Ignatius of Antioch to the Romans* (circa 117 CE). Ignatius, being escorted to Rome to face the emperor and certain execution, writes ahead to the Christian community at Rome: "Let me be food for the wild beasts, through whom I can reach God. I am God's wheat and I am being ground by the teeth of wild beasts, that I may prove to be pure bread . . . then I will truly be a disciple of Jesus Christ, when the world will no longer see my body."

These theologically charged reflections on the significance of the martyr's sacrifice were a kind of homily for a persecuted church: they became a "proof" of the meaning of the life of Jesus and a model for those discipleship instructions that were in the Gospel message.[6] The theme of the *imitatio Christi* found in these early documents would be a recurring theme in later martyrdom accounts. Finally, these texts hold up the martyrs as models and exemplars of faith which, of course, becomes one component in the development of their cult in subsequent history.

Later elaborations of these *Passiones* became more fictionalized as they exaggerated the sufferings of the martyrs, the demonic opposition of the Romans (and the Jews), and the miraculous powers of the saints to withstand pain, thwart the persecutors, and exhibit the presence of God's power among them. Such stories known as *legenda* (literally: matters read aloud) would evolve, as we shall see, into the tradition of hagiography.

Veneration

There is no doubt that those who did die for the sake of the faith were highly venerated in the Christian community. The literature that grew up about them is proof enough of that fact. A further proof is that when their bodies were recovered after execution they were given special attention both in terms of their burial and also in the honor paid to the places where they were interred. This custom has deep historical roots in the Christian tradition. The second-century text *The Martyrdom of Polycarp* notes that the witnesses to the saint's death buried his body in a suitable place with the hope that "the Lord will permit us, as far as possible, to gather together in joy and gladness to celebrate the day of his martyrdom as a birthday [*dies natalis*], in memory of those athletes who have gone before, and to train and make ready those who come thereafter."

The veneration of the martyrs at their tombs was an extension of the Roman custom of memorializing their dead on an annual basis. What was new in the practice of the Christians was to observe the date of the martyr's death as a "birthday," i.e. that day in which they were born anew into the realm of God. This veneration had a deep religious significance evidenced by the fact that the same *Martyrdom of Polycarp* was quick to point out to some Jews of Smyrna, who accused them of abandoning Christ, that they observed the cult of the martyrs "because of their unsurpassable devotion to their own King and Teacher" who were "disciples and imitators of the Lord."

As the list of martyrs became longer, the calendar of those commemorated also grew. Early liturgical texts indicate that observances at the tombs of the martyrs included readings (from the *Passiones*?), psalms and prayers, and possibly the celebration of the Eucharist. By the middle of the fourth century, we have a list of those martyrs who were commemorated in Rome on an annual basis (the so-called *Depositio Martyrum*) with similar lists compiled in cities like Antioch and Carthage. It is from this practice that, in time, there developed a cycle of saintly veneration that meshed with the larger liturgical cycle of the church. One scholar has pointed out that the Roman *Depositio Martyrum* begins, fittingly enough, on December 25 with the birthday of Jesus – the model for all Christian martyrs.[7]

From this slow evolution of the veneration of the martyrs certain other practices developed. Until the early fourth century, when Christianity gained its legitimacy and the persecutions ended, the martyrs were buried in Christian-maintained cemeteries. In Rome and a few other places, these cemeteries were cut as underground galleries in the soft volcanic rock known as *tufa* or, in the case of similar galleries in Sicily, quarry tunnels. Most of the many people buried in these cemeteries (known to us as "catacombs" which was originally the name of one such cemetery: *ad catacumbas*) died of natural causes. Those spots that housed martyrs were so marked. The periodic raids of barbarians from the north at the close of the late antique period led the Roman church authorities to re-bury the remains of martyrs inside the city walls in churches or shrine chapels erected for that purpose. When feasible, churches were built over the burial spots so that these ecclesiastical buildings also marked the catacombs.[8]

The Roman cemeteries fell into disuse for centuries. It was only in the sixteenth century that many of the underground galleries were rediscovered and explored, and it was well into the early nineteenth century that there was anything like a scientific archaeological methodology developed to understand the character and significance of these early burial places. Unfortunately, the sixteenth-century discovery of the catacombs gave rise to the notion that everyone buried in them had fallen during the Roman persecutions. This misapprehension and the added idea that Christians hid in the galleries of the catacombs and worshiped there in secret (they did hold services in the catacombs on the *dies natalis* of a martyr or in commemorative rites for family members) were reinforced in the nineteenth century by a plethora of romantic novels depicting life in the "church of the catacombs" (Newman's *Callista* is a fair example of the genre).

A particularly interesting case of fictional elaboration with respect to the martyrs occurred in the nineteenth century when a tomb was discovered in the catacombs of Priscilla in Rome with a somewhat garbled epitaph. It was understood to read "Peace to you Filumena." Inside the tomb was an ampulla thought to contain dried blood and some bones. These relics were transferred to the Italian town of Mugnano where Filomena was venerated as a virgin martyr (a pious priest even wrote a "biography") with miracles reported at her tomb shrine. Pius IX even authorized a mass and office to be established in her honor and Filomena soon became a favorite first name for young girls, especially in Italy. Only subsequently did research indicate that the archaeological evidence was tendentious at best. In 1961 the Vatican suppressed her feast day (August 11) and struck her name from the catalog of saints.

An even more curious case resulted from the shipment of some relics from a Roman catacomb to a religious house in Paris. Misreading the label on the box, the recipients translated *spedito* ("sent") as the saint's name, thus giving rise to the fictional military saint who was given the Latin name Expeditus who remained in the calendar of saints until modern times.

After Constantine

The emperor Constantine brought toleration for the Christians in the Roman empire with the Edict of Milan in AD 313, just a decade after one of the most ferocious periods of persecution under the emperor Diocletian which went on intermittently from AD 303 to the accession of Constantine to the imperial purple. In the period after Constantine, the veneration and liturgical of the sainted martyrs was a well-established part of Christian life. Constantine himself paid fair tribute to the practice by, among other things, underwriting the erection of a large basilica over the tomb of Saint Peter on the site of the shrine (*tropheum*) where his remains were venerated. A less-reliable tradition ascribes to Constantine the basilica of Saint Paul-outside-the-Walls over the remains of the apostle to the Gentiles.

One might well have expected the naming and veneration of saints to have ceased with the end of the Roman persecutions but an interesting shift took place. If one wanted to categorize the periods of Christian history by ideal types, then the first four centuries comprised the age of the martyrs, which was then replaced by the age of the ascetics and the monks. By the fourth century, the veneration of the martyrs had rooted itself in both the popular Christian practice of piety and in the emerging shape of the liturgical life of the church. Prayers and liturgies at the tombs of the martyrs were considered to be extremely efficacious and the bodies and other relics of the saints were thought to be loci of sacred power. The veneration of martyrs' relics had already been noted in the second-century *Martyrium Polycarpi*, where the remains of Polycarp were described as more precious than gems or gold. Both Saint Jerome and Saint Augustine would later argue for the legitimacy of such veneration.

Augustine, in his *Confessions*, famously describes his own mother, Monica, as a regular visitor to the shrine of the third-century martyr Saint Cyprian in Carthage. When Ambrose, bishop of Milan, discouraged such practices due to excesses, Augustine noted that Monica gave up the custom and now saw "the wisdom of bringing to the martyrs' shrines not a basket full of the fruits of the earth but a heart full of more purified offerings, her prayers" (*Confessions* VI: 2).

The natural successors of the martyred saints were the ascetics and monks.[9] In his classic *Life of Antony*, written in the fourth century, Athanasius says that Antony, through his life of solitary prayer and asceticism, was a "martyr every day of his life." Athanasius, of course, fully understood that the word "martyr" means a witness. Athanasius' *Life of Antony* had an enormous impact on the rise of monasticism. Augustine, in the *Confessions*, tells us how much his *Life* attracted young people who sought out the ascetic life. Antony was widely venerated in the Middle Ages, becoming the subject of any number of famous paintings which delighted in depicting the demonic temptations he suffered in the most vivid fashion. Hieronymus Bosch devoted a famous triptych to this subject, while Matthias Grünewald devoted a panel of his famous Isenheim altarpiece to the same subject. In the nineteenth century, Gustave Flaubert used the struggles of Antony to fuel his imaginative fictional portrait of the saint in his novel *La Tentation de St Antoine*.

In some now classic studies, Peter Brown has shown how these holy men and women of late antiquity were seen as conduits of divine power and resources of wisdom and healing. Their very lives were considered to exemplify the virtues, graces, and redemptive power of Christ himself who was the exemplar par excellence of the martyr and ascetic.[10]

Athanasius' *Life of Antony* was only the first of a whole spate of popular books on the great ascetics and monastics which appeared in late antiquity. Saint Jerome wrote a somewhat fanciful life of the first hermit, Paul of Thebes (died 340?), who was said to be a friend of Saint Antony of the Desert. The monastic founder Pachomius (died 346) inspired a number of lives which have come down to us both in Coptic and Greek. Saint Gregory of Nyssa wrote a life of his sister, Macrina, shortly after her death in 397. In the early fifth century, Palladius compiled his *Lausiac History*, chronicling the lives of the Egyptian monks of the Thebiad. A century later, Cyril of Scythopolis composed his *Lives of the Palestinian Monks*, drawing on his experiences as a monk in the environs of Jerusalem. Finally, while not strictly biographical, the "Sayings of the Desert Fathers" (*Apophthegmata*

Patrum), an alphabetical collection of the aphorisms, sayings, and spiritual advice of the desert fathers, compiled in the early sixth century but echoing an oral tradition that goes back into the fourth, has had a continuous and important influence on subsequent generations of Christians both in the East and the West. All of these works held up the ascetics as models of Christian witness.

Perhaps the most extravagant of the early ascetic saints were those who lived on platforms on pillars known as the *stylites*. Open to the weather, they not only devoted their lives to prayer but were famous for their spiritual advice. Attended by disciples who would send up food and other basic necessities, these ascetics lived, as it were, suspended between heaven and earth. They flourished in the Middle East and Greece well into the early Middle Ages. The purported founder of this tradition was the Syrian Saint Simeon Stylites (died *c*.459) who, after a conventional life as a monk, lived on an elevated platform until his death. He carried on a vast correspondence, attracted hordes of pilgrims and spiritual seekers (including many non-Christians), and inspired a monastery and church around his pillar, the remains of which can be seen to this day.

The writings about the lives of both martyrs and ascetics borrowed from earlier biblical and Hellenistic models of the biographies of exemplary figures. The Bible was an obvious source of inspiration where one could find narrative lives of figures such as Moses and Joseph. Furthermore, there were martyrdom templates to be found in such exemplary lives as those who died in defense of Judaism, such as Rabbi Eleazer (2 Macc. 6) and the pious Jewish mother and her seven sons whose martyrdom was described in 2 Maccabees 7. The Book of Ecclesiasticus (not considered canonical by the Reformation) has seven long chapters praising the ancestors of Judaism. In addition to these biblical sources, there were also the many aretologies and "lives of illustrious men" that were part of the pagan literary inheritance.[11]

In the post-Constantinian period it became quite common for people to travel in order to visit famous solitaries in their desert dwellings or, in not a few cases, to consult pillar-dwelling ascetics. With the support of Constantine's mother, Helena, not only was there a whole series of buildings and shrines constructed to commemorate the places in ancient Palestine associated with the life of Jesus but that same area became a magnet for those seeking the solitary life. The pilgrimage treatise of the Spanish holy woman, Egeria, written in the late fourth century, narrates her long trip through Egypt, the Holy Land, Edessa, Asia Minor, and Constantinople. A crucial resource for understanding the fourth-century liturgy in Jerusalem, it is also valuable as she frequently notes the presence of ascetics and monks of both sexes who lived in the areas she visited.

In the West, the most famous saint of the late fourth century was Martin of Tours (died c.397). Born in Hungary, he abandoned his life as a soldier and, after a period as a hermit, he entered the monastic life with Hilary of Poitiers. Famous for his ascetic life and his power as a healer, his biography was written by his disciple Sulpicius Severus while Martin was still alive. That *Vita* became so popular that it served as a kind of model for hagiographical writing well into the Middle Ages and contributed to the cult of Martin who became one of the favored saints of Europe.[12] Four thousand parish churches in France alone were dedicated to him (as well as five hundred villages which bore his name). Pilgrimages to his shrine in Tours were popular well into the sixteenth century. Interestingly enough, the life of Martin strongly emphasized the saint's miraculous powers, comparing him favorably to the exemplary ascetics of the Egyptian deserts.

There was nothing like any formal canonization process in the first millennium of Christian history. Veneration of the saints developed from the ground up and usually followed a typical pattern. A certain person was conspicuous for ascetic practices, wise counsel, heroic fidelity to prayer, and, most of all, thaumaturgical powers. Such a person was sought out during his or her lifetime. When the person died, the person's grave site became a place of prayer. If such a practice persisted, a shrine was built over the tomb or the body was relocated to a church. People would come for private devotions and the shrine place came under the protection of monastic or clerical guardianship. In connection with the shrine place, it would be natural enough to have special pilgrimages on the anniversary of the person's death.

If there was one central element in the continuation of a cult in favor of the saints it was to be found in their ability to performs miracles in their lifetime and, more importantly, after their death. Their shrines provided a link between the earthly and the heavenly. Their place in heaven was a pledge of what those on earth could hope to gain. Writing in the fifth century, Saint Maximus of Turin put the latter succinctly: "All the martyrs are to be honored by us especially in this life and especially those whose relics we possess; they preserve us in our bodies in this life and receive us when we depart hence."

In this central role of the power of the saints to aid those on earth by saintly intervention, it is worthwhile to note the work of the sixth-century bishop of Rome, Gregory the Great (died 604). A prolific writer, often called the last of the Western Fathers, Gregory wrote a rather prolix work about 593 known as *The Dialogues*. In this work, divided into four books, Gregory recounts the lives and miracles of a number of saints who lived in Italy to show that the miraculous was still flourishing in the Italy of his day. *The Dialogues'* greatest claim to fame is to be found in Book II, which is the only source we have for the life of Saint Benedict of Nursia, now regarded as the founder of Western monasticism. *The Dialogues* was one of the most read books of the Middle Ages (it was at least partially inspired by Sulpicius Severus' earlier life of Martin of Tours). What is most interesting about it for our story is that one of its purposes was to argue that great sanctity and the presence of the miraculous had not died out in previous times but was still very much alive in the works of the saints which Gregory described in his work.

Gregory's *Dialogues* also shows a fascination for and an understanding of the power inherent in the relics of the saints. Gregory's interlocutor in the *Dialogues* ask why relics sometimes are the occasion of greater miracles than those performed at the tomb of a saint. Gregory explains that a person praying before distant relics of a saint "earns all the more merit by his faith, for he realizes that the martyrs are present to hear his prayers even though their bodies happened to be buried elsewhere."[13]

It was the same pope Gregory who sent the monk Augustine to England to evangelize the island. In 601, four years after Augustine began his missionary work, Gregory sent the monk Mellitus to assist in the task of evangelization. In a letter recorded in Bede's eighth-century *A History of the English Church and People*, Gregory suggested a missionary strategy that sheds some light on the cult of the saints in relation to the pagan past of Europe. Gregory tells Mellitus that when they come across pagan temples the idols are to be smashed but the temples themselves are to be re-consecrated for Christian use with altars to be set up and relics of the saints set into the former temples (presumably into the altars themselves). Furthermore, if there has been a custom of sacrificing animals on a certain day in honor of the pagan idols, those days should be changed: "Let some other solemnity be substituted in its place, such as a day of Dedication or the Festivals of the holy martyrs whose relics are enshrined there" (Book I, chapter 30).

The interesting thing about this pastoral advice is that it helps us to put the widespread popularity of the cult of the saints into some kind of cultural context. The ancient world was a world that was alive with powers, forces, spirits, and gods. It was a world saturated in the spiritual. In a sense, the cult of the saints was a form of replacement for the powers of various pagan tutelaries and gods. The healing shrines, the sacred wells, the temples of the members of the pagan pantheon had now been replaced by the power of the saints who had overcome these pagan divinities and sublunar powers. The fact that Christianity was spreading did not in any way erase the older conviction that the wall between the visible and the spiritual was rather permeable.

There was always the danger (and sometimes the danger was realized) that the saints would simply become new names for old pagan divinities and that the search for miracles would degenerate into magical practices. This was a fear expressed as late as Erasmus's *The Praise of Folly* in the sixteenth century (and made much of in the polemics of the Reformation), but it was not something about which the patristic church was insensitive. Augustine of Hippo's massive work *The City of God* was centrally concerned with the struggle between paganism and Christianity. In the final book (XXII) of that work, Augustine takes up the issue of miracles done through the intercession of the martyrs both to argue that such miracles had in fact taken place and, further, that they were a sign of approval and a further proof of the redemptive work of Christ. He was so convinced of this that, as he says, he had such accounts of favors received through the intercession of the saints read out to his congregation in Hippo. (The word "legend" originally meant something read aloud; from the Latin *legere* = to read.) Augustine further stipulated that there was no similarity between the works of the saints and those of the pagan divinities:

> We do not in those shrines raise altars on which to sacrifice to the martyrs but to the one God who is the martyrs' God and ours; and at this sacrifice the martyrs are named in their own place and in the appointed order, as men of God who have overcome the world in God's name. They are not invoked by the priest who offers sacrifice. He is offering the sacrifice to God and not to the martyrs. (Book XXII, chapter 10)

The saints, in short, were not to be adored; they were invoked as intercessors because they were already where all Christians hope to be: before the throne of God.

The one thing that emerges clearly from this rapid survey is that, by the waning years of the late antique period, the cult of the saints was already well lodged in the practice of Christianity. Born out of the experience of martyrdom, and furthered by the example of the ascetics and the spread of the monastic life, the veneration of the saints was part of the fabric of Christian piety.

In the late antique and early medieval period there was no formal procedure by which one entered the list (canon) of the saints. All that was required to achieve the reputation of being a saint after death was a body or something identified with the person to be venerated, a shrine of some sort, a narrative of the person's life and deeds (it could be something as brief as the acts of the person's condemnation in the case of a martyr), and people who would come to pray at the place where the shrine was located. The overarching criterion marking the desirability of such signs was a continuing indication of the miraculous. The most formal recognition that a person could hope for in addition to those conditions was being placed in the calendar(s) of those who were commemorated publicly in the liturgy of the great centers of the church like Rome or Jerusalem.

One natural consequence of the importance attached to the attractive power of such sacred places where the saints were at rest was that it generated that most persistent of religious activities, already in the late antique period and continuous to the present day: pilgrimage. In the Irish church it was the rare saint, after the time of Patrick, who did not make at least one pilgrimage to Rome with an almost obligatory stop at Tours in Gaul to honor Saint Martin. Pilgrimage was both a penitential exercise imposed at times on a sinner and an ascetical exercise undertaken by monks. For the poor farmer, who could not absent himself for a long trip to Rome, there was always the local shrine or monastic center where one could go and seek the intervention of the saints and the relics there held.[14] Pilgrimage became so popular in the early medieval period that some of the spiritual writers had to warn about its purely secular popularity; hence the famous Irish poem: "Going to Rome / is lots of effort, little profit. / You won't find the king you seek there / unless you take him along."

Chapter 2

The Bureaucratization of Sanctity

Saints should be judged guilty until proven innocent.

George Orwell

Liturgical Memory of the Saints

By the end of the fourth century, and certainly well into the fifth, the saints were recalled by name and/or class in the central act of Christian worship, the Eucharistic liturgy. This recollection occurred not only for the keeping of saints' days but also found expression in the formal ordinary liturgical texts used in worship. In the Byzantine world, the Sunday liturgy was normally celebrated according to a rite ascribed to Saint John Chrysostom (347–407), which to this day is used on all but ten Sundays of the year in both the Greek and Russian Churches. After the consecration of the bread and the wine, the celebrant "offers this reasonable service for those who rest in faith, the fathers, patriarchs, prophets, apostles, preachers, evangelists, martyrs, confessors, ascetics and all the righteous perfected in faith"; then, in a louder voice, the priest continues: "especially our all-holy, immaculate, highly glorious, blessed lady, Mother of God and ever-virgin Mary; Saint John the forerunner and Baptist, and the holy and honored apostles; and this saint whose memorial we are keeping [i.e. the saint commemorated on that day]; at those entreaties, look upon us, O Lord."

In the Roman rite for the mass, whose origins also go back to the fifth century, the celebrant asks God to remember those who stand in the church who are "In fellowship with and venerating the memory" of "the glorious and ever Virgin Mary, Mother of Our God and Lord Jesus Christ, and also your blessed apostles and martyrs [here the apostles and Roman martyrs are called by name] and all your saints, by whose merits and prayers grant us to be defended in all things by the help of your protection . . ." After the consecration of the bread and wine, the celebrant then prays that those who celebrate the liturgy will be granted "some part and fellowship with your holy apostles and martyrs, with John, Stephen, Matthias, Barnabas, Ignatius, Alexander, Marcellinus, Peter, Felicity, Perpetua, Agatha, Lucy, Agnes, Cecilia, Anastasia, and with all your saints . . ." Those commemorations are still used in the first of the four Eucharistic prayers found in the reformed liturgy of the post-Vatican II Roman Catholic Church.

The liturgical insistence that the community at worship is in the company of all the saints, from the Old Testament figures onwards, finds its most visual representation in the art of the church. To go into a Byzantine church is to be confronted by the iconostasis with its complex series of icons; typically, the walls of the church are also decorated. Using a different style of decoration, churches in the West have stained-glass windows, pictures, and statues in the apse, and ancillary altars, also depicting the range of the saints. One of the most striking churches exemplifying this notion of the entire church at worship is the fifth-century basilica of Sant'Apollinare Nuovo in Ravenna, Italy. On both walls of the nave, below the clerestory, are continuous mosaics of sainted martyrs, men on one side and women on the other, in procession towards the main altar. When a person entered the church for worship it was, as it were, as if the communicant were joining some vast procession of saints who were

Plate 1 Procession of saints in the Church of Sant'Apollinare Nuovo in Ravenna, Italy. Photo © 1990 SCALA, Florence, courtesy of the Ministero Beni e Att. Culturali.

moving in the same direction as the worshiper looking towards the altar.

Similar kinds of commemorations are to be found in varying degrees of specificity in the other ancient liturgies of both the East and the West. Some things are worthy of note, however, in the brief excerpts cited above. First, the Christian church understands the saints, named and unnamed, to be part of the larger company of the Holy Ones who go back all the way in history to the patriarchs and matriarchs of the Old Testament. Second, the liturgy sees the company of the saints as part of the whole church made most vibrant within the worship of the church itself. Third, there is already an apparent ranking of the saints in terms of the honor given them: the Virgin Mary, John the Baptist, the apostles; then the martyrs, confessors, ascetics, and so on. Finally, one can detect in the language of the liturgy the theological understanding that the church expresses in its official liturgy: the saints are a sign of hope for Christians who will some day join them with God; next, they are a part of the fellowship of all who are in the church; finally, through their prayers, they are intercessors before God in heaven. There is, then, a kind of eschatological strain attached to the veneration of the saints, most conspicuously in the liturgy. We pray in union with all the saints in anticipation of the day when all will be joined together before the throne of God.

The liturgy tends to conserve the most authentic theological understanding of the Christian faith (*lex orandi / lex credendi* is the old expression to encapsulate that truth), but the history of the saints also has possessed a lush (and sometimes uncontrolled) popular piety which has not always kept close to the formal liturgical life of the ancient church; indeed, it grew alongside (and not always in harmony with) the official liturgy. That popular piety was to be the concern of the reforming elements of the church in many and various ways, as we shall see.

The Saintly Legend

As we have already seen, the oldest literature about the martyrs are those relatively few *Acta* that are more or less accurate records of the Roman judicial proceedings. These are typically limited to the personal affirmation of faith together with a refusal to worship the pagan gods and the subsequent condemnation to death. The *Passio* is a more articulated text, written under Christian auspices, for the purpose both of edifying the Christian community and of acting as a circular letter to allow other communities to know how the martyr(s) remained steadfast in the fidelity to Christ. The *Passio* typically has a "thicker" rhetorical overlay with scriptural allusions, hortatory interventions, and so on. The *Martyrium Polycarpi*, discussed in chapter 1, is exemplary of the type, although we have many other texts that fit the category.

The *legendum* (plural *legenda*) is a expanded story of the saint, often used at feasts at the shrine of a saint or a martyr, but also frequently improvised to exalt the heroic virtues of the saint and his or her patient sufferings under tortures, as well as the miraculous elements attached to the saint's life and the power of the saint's relics after death. What one finds quite frequently, in the analysis of saint's lives, is the tendency to "fill in the blanks." A particular place may possess the tomb of a martyr or some other holy person, but there is no knowledge of that person beyond his or her name and general reputation. There is an almost reactive tendency to flesh out that person's story even if few facts are known. Not infrequently, part of that fleshing out consists of adding fictive miracles or folktales or gleanings from popular romances.

At other times, especially in the case of the personae of the New Testament, the "filling in of the blanks" consisted of naming anonymous players in the Gospel story who could make a fair claim to sanctity. Luke tells us that certain women lamented as Jesus carried his cross to Golgotha (Luke 23: 27–31). An early medieval story named one of these women who, it was said, offered a cloth to wipe the face of Jesus which then resulted in a portrait on the cloth (kept as a relic in Saint Peter's basilica in Rome). Her name was given as Veronica (*vera* + *ikon* = "true image"), and she now has a place in the popular exercise of the Stations of the Cross. Similarly, the good thief (Luke 23: 39–43), who was crucified with Christ, received the name "Dismas" in an early non-canonical gospel based, probably, on the Greek word *dusme* (dying). The same sources name the unrepentant thief as "Gestas." Saint Dismas is now honored as the patron saint of convicts.

Saintly legends grew apace from the late antique period through the Anglo-Saxon and Celtic traditions and into, and beyond, the Carolingian era. Certain saints "traveled" as their stories and putative relics moved along trade routes, accompanied missionary journeys, and military excursions. Thus, to cite a conspicuous example, devotion to the fourth-century Saint Nicholas of Myra (in present-day Turkey) spread to the West through the port city of Bari in southern Italy in the tenth century and north in subsequent centuries into places as disparate as the British Isles and Russia. Devotion to the saint in the Low Countries became blended with Nordic folktales, transforming this early Greek bishop into that Christmas icon, Santa Claus.[1] Likewise, the cult of the sixth-century Irish Saint Brigid of Kildare, who was head of a double monastery of men and women and about whom many elements of druidic customs accrued, was honored in Italy because a ninth-century Irish pilgrim, Bishop Donatus of Fiesole (near Florence) introduced her cult there and also wrote her life in Latin hexameters. Another Irishman, Sedulius Scotus (Scotus = Irishman), introduced her cult in Liège (in Belgium) from where her cult spread to Austria, Germany, and Brittany. In Ireland itself, after her death, the nuns of Kildare kept a fire burning at the place of her death for many centuries, possibly carrying on a custom of female druids before the time of Christianity.

The most famous compilation of such legends (both Brigid and Nicholas appear in it) was the *Legenda Sanctorum* (which soon became known as *The Golden Legend* – the *Legenda Aurea*), compiled around 1260 by the Dominican friar Jacobus de Voragine (?1230–1298). That work drew upon many earlier stories, folktales, exempla, and pious elaborations dating into the early Middle Ages. Most likely meant to be of use to preachers, it was an enormously popular work with over a thousand manuscript copies surviving from the Middle Ages with many editions translated from its original Latin. It was one of the first books printed by the fifteenth-century English publisher William Caxton, who produced an English version in 1483. No other book was reprinted more often between 1470 and 1530, and over one hundred different editions in a wide sweep of languages have been noted. Any person who peruses this enormously influential work will find in it a farrago of improbable, and not always edifying, miraculous stories with some of such exaggeration that Jacobus himself was forced to admit that some of what he reported was probably not true. However much it may be a work of less historical worth, it is a crucial text for translating the allusions in homilies, particular lives of the saints, and the religious iconography of the times.[2]

The *legenda*, in many cases, were the written record of stories, fanciful etymologies, folktales, and exempla which had agglutinated into a (fanciful) whole. There has been a scholarly industry, going back into the seventeenth century, attempting to untangle such stories and looking for a possible historical core. Quite frequently, a legend will reflect layers of accretions over the ages. The case of the patron saint of travelers, Saint Christopher, is a good case in point. From an early cultus in both the Western and Eastern churches, honoring a third-century martyr who died during the persecution of Decius, a tradition arose that he was an exceptionally tall or strong man (in some tellings of the story, he was transformed into a giant), who once served Satan before his conversion. According to *The Golden Legend*, he was a ferryman who took travelers across a river ford. While carrying a child who was so heavy that Christopher almost sank, it was revealed that the child was Christ who carried human sins. Hence the name Christopher (from the Greek for "Christ bearer") and the popular image of a husky man with a child on his shoulders. In the late Middle Ages his image was painted on the outside of churches with the popular belief that whoever looked on his image would not die that day. He was also the patron saint of travelers, which explains the ubiquitous medallions which once festooned the inside of automobiles. Despite his appeal in popular religion, his name was removed from the universal calendar of the saints by the Roman Catholic Church in 1969, but his anniversary may be observed locally.

A similar series of accretions can be seen in the development of the cult of Saint George, who is known as the "great martyr" in the Orthodox world. A martyr who died in the early fourth century, his legend grew in the sixth century, and by the twelfth century he was reputed to be a dragon-slayer (based on the story of Perseus slaying the sea monster in Greek mythology?). Saint George was particularly venerated in the British Isles, with soldiers and sailors wearing his colors (white with a red cross) from the fourteenth century on. He was named the patron of England in the same century probably due to his connection to the founding of the Order of the Garter. In the Christian East, Saint George is often associated with other saints, like Saints Demetrius and Theodore, who are known as the "soldier saints."

It is not difficult to see how such stories could arise. The cult of the saints had, until the early Middle Ages, a certain ad hoc quality about them. What constituted a saint, basically, was reputation in life and, more importantly, a cultus around the saint's tomb. That cultus, in turn, depended on the regularity of evidence of cures, healings, and favors granted through the intercession of the saint. A good deal of that "evidence" was the product of an oral culture. It was in the interest of those who maintained the shrine to have a record of miracles. In certain places, a secretary was at hand to record various "favors" or "healings." It was not uncommon for relics to be stolen and translated to another spot to enhance the aura of the miraculous of a given place.[3] Quite often, the fundamental function of colleges of clergy or monastic communities, apart from their own spiritual life, was to act as custodians of relics and serve as monitors of the devotional life around the saint's shrine. It is well to remember that the greatest prestige that the bishops of Rome enjoyed in the early centuries of Christianity accrued to them precisely because they were guardians of the tombs of Saints Peter and Paul. Scholars of Irish monasticism point out that the round monastic enclosures consisted of rings. The outer ring was open to lay persons; the second ring was reserved for clerics; in the center ring was the "holy of holies" within which (preferably) the body of the sainted founder and other relics of the saints were kept. The presence of the saint's relics was what made the settlement a holy place.[4]

The *legenda* also served the further purpose of providing a resource for preachers who urged a faithful life, for lay readers (a minority) who wished to be edified by the virtues of the saints, and as a continuing apologetic proof that both saintliness and the power that saintliness brought were still palpable in our world. Indeed, there is a distinct genre of writings, drawing on the sayings of holy men and women, which does not emphasize the miraculous but, rather, the spiritual teachings of heroic saints. The influential writings of Saint John Cassian (?360–433) are an illustration of this attempt at edification. His *Conferences* report on his conversations with the great ascetics of the Egyptian desert but hardly mention their miraculous powers. His *Institutes* (which had an enormous influence on monasticism) do not mention the miraculous. As he says in his preface to that volume, he will omit such matters since such things "minister to the reader nothing but astonishment and no instruction about the perfect life." Evidently, Cassian wrote the *Institutes* to describe the formal lives of the monks and the *Conferences* to elucidate their interior lives of piety. What he decided to omit, however, was any extended discussion of the miraculous.

Regularizing Sainthood

It was inevitable that, as Europe emerged from the dark ages after the dissolution of the post-Carolingian period, along with the emergence of city life, the sporadic efforts to reform the church, the greater ease of travel, and the increase in economic life, attempts to regularize the cult of the saints would also gain the attention of church authority. This was not a quick process. Before the high Middle Ages, there was no systematic set of procedures for canonization. By "canonization" is meant a process by which a person is inscribed on the list (Greek: *kanon*) of those to whom liturgical honors are paid either at the local (for example, the saint of this or that monastery or diocese) or universal level. While the church believed that everyone who died in God's grace was in heaven, canonization singled out from the general mass of the faithful certain iconic figures who represented the "best" of the faithful and the most reliable persons who might intercede for people before the throne of God.

From roughly the sixth to the tenth century, what formal canonizations took place did so under the supervision of the local bishop. The process *qua* process was rather informal. A petition would be made to the bishop, usually accompanied by a written text about the putative saint's life and merits. If the bishop was suitably convinced, permission was given to transfer the body of the saint (the transfer – *translatio* – had a highly symbolic value and was, in places, also commemorated as a feast day in its own right) to a suitable shrine location and a festival date set to be added to the calendar of the saints (the so-called *sanctorale*). They were, in effect, inscribed on the list (*kanon*) of those who could be venerated. As might be imagined, the number of regional *sanctorales* tended to multiply without any central organization.

Today, in the Roman Catholic Church, canonizations fall under the sole competence of papal authority. How that centralization of canonization authority happened involves a long historical story. The Roman Church had a well-developed cycle of saints' feast days that was well in place by the sixth century. That cycle of feasts honored, in the main, martyrs and confessors who were either identified with the city and its environs or figures of universal significance, such as those associated with Christ (for example, John the Baptist and the apostles). By the end of the fifth century the city was dotted with churches dedicated to the memory of the great Roman martyrs as well as the apostles and some conspicuous confessors. During Lent, daily services were held at the "stational" churches of a given saint.[5] The last saint, before the eleventh century, to enter into the Roman calendar was Pope Saint Gregory the Great who died in 604.

It was not until the early eleventh century that new saints were added to the Roman calendar. Pope Gregory VII added thirty popes from the ancient church to the calendar as part of his strategy of enhancing the power of the papacy. In 1173 he added the name of the Englishman, Saint Thomas Becket, who had been assassinated by the king's courtiers three years earlier and was already the focus of an intense cult in England. Interestingly enough, he is listed as a martyr even though it is clear that the king's partisans killed him because of his resistance to monarchical power. When Thomas Becket's name was enrolled in the Roman canon of saints the last saint to be put on the list before him was Gregory the Great who had lived nearly six hundred years earlier.

The actual jurisprudential procedures for canonization proceeded by long steps. The earliest saint to be canonized for whom we have an actual dossier is Saint Ulrich of Augsburg, who was canonized by Pope John XV in 993. Ulrich was best known for his work as a bishop and his rebuilding of his episcopal city after it had been ravaged by the then-pagan Magyars. In his old age he retired to the famous monastery of Saint Gall in Switzerland.

The *Decretals* of Pope Gregory IX, promulgated in 1234, stipulated that no person was to be canonized without the authority of the pope. By the early fourteenth century, a formal legal process of investigation was established before such a canonization would take place. Thus, when looking at the long lists of saints honored in the church, one must distinguish between those who have been formally canonized according to the jurisprudence of the Roman curia and those who are so honored by long custom. Many of the greatest saints in the church (for example, Saint Augustine) have never been formally canonized in the sense that we understand the term today. Nor are the categories always observed in a rigid pattern. Pope Victor III (1027–1087) is invoked as a saint at the Abbey of Monte Cassino, but he bears only the title of "Blessed" in the martyrology of the universal church. The process itself was a slow one, and canonizations were not frequent at the papal level. The last English saint to be canonized before the Reformation was Saint John of Bridlington (died 1379), who was canonized by Pope Boniface IX in 1401.

A Test Case: Francis of Assisi

We can get some sense of the medieval process of papal canonization by looking at the case of Saint Francis of Assisi. Francis is a good example since we possess a clear set of documents which helps us to understand how papal canonizations proceeded.

Francis of Assisi was one of the most popular saints of the Middle Ages, a popularity which extends into our own day as clearly evidenced by the huge streams of pilgrims and tourists who come to the picturesque Umbrian town where he is buried. It was in Assisi that Pope John Paul II convoked two large interreligious gatherings of religious representatives from the world's many religions since Assisi, associated with the saint, seemed the most appropriate place for such historic encounters.

When Francis died in 1226 at a relatively young age (he was born in 1181 or 1182) he was already considered a saint by many people. Francis had attracted to his way of life a large number who wanted to live as a "lesser brother" as he called himself and his companions. Less than a decade before his death, his friars, thought then to have numbered three thousand, had gathered at Assisi. These friars had already spread to the British Isles and to Hungary. Some of them had died as martyrs in Morocco in their attempt to preach the gospel to Muslims. Assisi housed a large convent of nuns under the guidance of Francis's friend and soul mate, Clare of Assisi, and many lay people had remained in their own villages and towns but attempted to live a life prescribed for such members of his "third order."

A year after Francis died, Hugolino dei Conti di Segni, a nephew of the late Pope Innocent III and himself a cardinal, was elected

Plate 2 Saint Francis of Assisi (?1181–1226). Photo Stefan Diller / AKG-Images.

to the papacy, taking the name of Gregory IX. He had known Francis and had served as the cardinal protector of the Franciscan Order. Almost immediately after his installation as pope, Gregory did two things that put the canonization of Francis on the fast track: he ordered a life of Francis to be written and he issued a papal bull (from the Latin *bulla* meaning a seal) on April 29, 1228 asking the faithful to contribute alms in order to construct a special church in Assisi to hold the saint's body. On July 16 of the same year, Gregory went to Assisi and solemnly inscribed Francis in the canon of the saints. Three days later, in the nearby city of Perugia, he issued a second bull titled from its first three words, *Mira Circa Nos*, which constituted the actual formal declaration of canonization. October 4, the date of the saint's death, was designated as his feast day.

Towards the end of the papal bull Gregory concludes that, because he had known the saint well and because he had been convinced "by reliable witnesses of his many splendid miracles," we can be confident that the faithful "will be helped by his prayers and that we will have a patron in heaven who was our close friend on earth" and that "we [i.e. the pope] have decided to inscribe him as worthy of veneration in the catalog of the saints." In that short, penultimate paragraph are the essentials: his life was known as one of outstanding piety; his miracles testify to his holiness; he is worthy to serve as a patron in heaven and will act as a worthy intercessor.

In the following year the same pope wrote to the bishops of the world asking them to foster devotion to the saint. Then, on February 25, 1229, Gregory gave official approval to the *Life of Saint Francis*, written by the friar Thomas of Celano, and ordered it to be published. This was the first of many such lives that would be written in the thirteenth century, including others by Thomas of Celano himself. It is interesting to note that this first life took as its literary model the life of Saint Martin of Tours which had been written centuries earlier by Sulpicius Severus. It is also worthwhile to note that Thomas of Celano would refashion his life of the saint into a particular form so that chapters of it could be read in the liturgical services of Matins for the feast and octave celebrations in honor of the saint. This genre (called *Ad Usum Chori*, "for use in the choir") points to the importance of the liturgical veneration of saints over and beyond popular veneration associated with pilgrimages and private veneration at a saint's shrine.

It is outside the scope of this study to make more than passing comment, but it should be observed that hagiographical writings can have a polemical edge to them. This is particularly true in the case of the literature written about Francis in the thirteenth century. Various *vitae* were composed to demonstrate a particular aspect of the mind of Francis on a range of issues but especially on Francis's emphasis on radical poverty. The discussion about the mind of Francis caused deep rifts within the Franciscan family. The debate was so intensely divisive that, at a general chapter meeting of the order held in Narbonne in 1260, the general of the Franciscans, Bonaventure, was ordered to write a new life of the saint which would take on an official character. That Major Life (*Legenda Major*) was approved three years later and the other lives were suppressed (many of them not recovered until the nineteenth century). The recovery of those texts and discussions about their interrelationship have triggered a debate – the so-called "Franciscan Question" – which goes on to this day.[6]

From this brief excursus on the canonization of Saint Francis we can detect the general mode used in papal canonizations: the gathering of testimony about the person's sanctity and the evidence of the saint's miraculous powers both in life and after death; the solemn burial (often involving a transfer of the body – the so-called *translatio*) and erection of a shrine tomb; the development of a written life of the saint; the establishment of a liturgical office; and a set date for the observance of the saint's feast. This was and is a standard pattern in the practice of the Roman Catholic Church. The series of frescos (once attributed to Giotto) illustrating the life of the saint done in the thirteenth century for the upper church of the basilica of Saint Francis provided a visual counterpart to the many *legenda* written in the three generations after the saint's death.

While the process of canonization put an official "seal of approval" on the life of Francis, far more important was the impact he had on others who attempted to follow his example. Clare of Assisi (died 1253) was associated with Francis in his own lifetime. She fought during her life for the "privilege of poverty" so that her sisters could live without using endowments for income. She was an esteemed spiritual director and a confidante of popes. Others, like Saint Antony of Padua (died 1231), knew Francis and from him received encouragement for study and preaching at which he excelled. Today he is venerated as an apostle of the poor with many places taking contributions to pay for "Saint Antony's bread" for the poor. Antony's popularity as a saint was partially due to the preaching of another Franciscan saint, the wildly successful "revival" preacher, Saint Bernardino of Siena (died 1444) who held up Antony as a model. Saint Bonaventure, who died in the same year as Thomas Aquinas (1274), is often called the "second founder" of the Franciscan order. A learned theologian, he wrote the major life of Francis which became the canonical account of the saint's life for centuries. The story is told of him that when the legates came to tell him that the pope had made him a cardinal, they found him washing dishes after supper – a task he insisted on finishing before he received the news.

Other saints who came under Franciscan influence were the many women who took up the Franciscan style of life without actually taking religious vows. They affiliated themselves to the so-called "third orders." Margaret of Cortona, for instance, turned away from a common law relationship when her lover and their child were killed. She went back to her native city and lived an ascetical life with a special dedication to the sick poor. When she died in 1297 she was already considered a living saint by her fellow citizens.

In the Middle Ages, the phenomenon of women dwelling in urban areas as ascetics who were inspired by the burgeoning spiritualities of the Franciscans and other mendicant movements was widespread. Some, like Catherine of Siena, a Dominican tertiary in the fourteenth century, assumed prophetic stances in chiding ecclesiastical powers to move to reform, while others, like the fifteenth-century Saint Frances of Rome, gathered like-minded women together (mainly widows) to lead a life of service to the poor while being nourished by a given spirituality (in Frances's case, the Rule of Benedict). These women can be understood as precursors of the active religious communities of women who would become a hallmark of the modern church.

The Christian East

The veneration of saints, the honoring of their relics, and their depiction on the holy icons have been a part of Orthodox Christianity from its earliest beginnings. To this day in the Eucharistic liturgy the priest places nine pieces of bread on the paten used in the liturgy to represent the whole range of the saints: John the Baptist, the prophets of the Old Testament, the apostles, the holy hierarchs, martyrs, ascetics, unmercenary healers (i.e. the saints who were doctors, like Cosmas and Damien, who never charged money to heal), the ancestors of Christ, and the saint whose feast is commemorated on that day.

In the first millennium, saints were recognized as such by an informal method which developed from the ground up: the growth of a cult through popular veneration; the creation of a tradition of icons and *legenda*; the evidence of miracles; and liturgical recognition in churches and monasteries. The earliest evidence that we have of formal canonization (Greek: *anagnorisis*, "recognition") occurs only in the thirteenth century when canonizations were done by decree of the Holy Synod and the Patriarch of Constantinople. This more bureaucratic process, accompanied by a demand for evidence of the miraculous, may well have developed as a result of renewed contacts (not always happy contacts) between Constantinople and the church of the West. A fourteenth-century text does not disapprove of local liturgical celebration (for example, in the monasteries of Mount

Athos), but such a saint would not be celebrated in the Great Church of Hagia Sophia, the seat of the Patriarch, except by synodal decree. The Byzantine East, then, had (and still has) a bit more flexibility than the Western church since it both recognizes the legitimacy of local observation and canonization by synodal decree. This practice is also observed in the Russian Church. In contrast to the Western tendency to canonize many saints, the Orthodox East has been more parsimonious in its willingness to expand the list of canonized saints.[7] When such saints are so "recognized" it typically happens through synodal decree.

It should be noted in passing that the Western church had, in the past, allowed a certain regional autonomy in the matter of the saints even after the canonization process was centralized in Rome. For example, Saint Rita of Cascia (died 1457), the Augustinian visionary ascetic and bearer of the stigmata, enjoyed a fervent cult in her native area where she was buried in an ornate tomb, with accompanying letters from the local bishop lauding her sanctity and permitting prayers in her honor. It was only in 1900, however, that she was formally canonized in Rome (she had been beatified in 1626 after a flurry of reports about miracles through her intercession). Her body was transferred to a new basilica built in her honor in 1946 where her remains are visited by devout pilgrims. Her case is not absolutely singular.

Apart from the vast literature of lives of the saints produced over the centuries, we can mention some "standard" works on the saints used in the Byzantine world which are connected to the liturgical celebrations honoring the saints. These can be briefly described. The *Menaion* contains hymns and prayers for the celebrations of the feast days of the saints. The *Menologion* is a collection of the lives of the saints and, in some cases, selected homilies honoring the saint, organized for each month of the year. The entries for a given saint may be read at the liturgy in addition to the prayers found in the *Menaion*. The *Synaxarion* is a compilation of brief notices of saints and where they are honored, as well as the details of their martyrdom. Often these notices were incorporated into the *Menaion*. The *Synaxarion* is quite similar to the Roman martyrology which, constantly updated, lists by day and month all the saints venerated in the Roman Catholic Church.

The Many Meanings of the Saints

It would be overly reductionist to think of the saints as only vehicles for the miraculous, even though the saint as a locus of sacred power before and after death is a persistent theme in the tradition of the saints. Saints were also models to be emulated. As early as the first martyrdom literature, the writers took pains to point out how the martyrs were imitators of Christ and models of steadfastness in faith and perseverance even to death. Athanasius ends his classic life of Antony, who, as we have seen, was praised as a martyr every day of his life, by holding up his life both as a template for "what the life of the monk ought to be" (cap. 94) and, further, as a persuasive example to pagans that the demons are not gods as they believe but evil forces overcome by the triumph of Christ. In that latter sense, it is clear that Athanasius saw the life of Antony as having an apologetic value. Readers of Saint Augustine's *Confessions* will remember how much Athanasius' *Life of Antony* meant to Augustine and his circle of intellectual aristocrats. "We were stupified," Augustine wrote, "as we listened to the tale of wonders you had worked within the true faith of the Catholic Church especially as they were most firmly attested by recent memory and had occurred so near our own time" (VIII. 14).

Saints were also considered to be patrons in heaven. In a feudal society, in which there was a strong hierarchical structure of class dependent on class, to have a patron (the local lord, the beneficent landowner, the prince or king) was to enjoy protection. That notion of patron was extended to the saint, who now stood as an intercessor in heaven. This emphasis on the patron gave rise to the widespread custom of designating a particular saint to be the patron of a given occupation (Saint Crispin for shoemakers; Saints Cosmas and Damien for physicians; Saint George for warriors, and so on) or to be invoked in case of a particular need (Saint Apollonia for toothache). Guilds, towns, fraternal organizations, and farms all had their particular patrons. Parishes were named for particular saints, and well into our own day children would choose an additional patron saint's name at the time of their confirmation.

Many saints were held up as models of Christian virtue and practice; in other words, their personae were as important for the lessons they exemplified as for their thaumaturgical capacities. The medieval canon of saints includes any number of kings and queens who serve as models of Christian leadership, just as model prelates, monks, and nuns are templates of authentic holiness. Even simple lay people (rarely) were canonized for their holy lives, such as the simple Saint Omobono (died 1197) of Cremona. Omobono was a married businessman who devoted himself to his family but also was centrally concerned with the needs of the poor. His rapid canonization (two years after his death) is almost without parallel in the medieval period where the distinguished path of holiness was to be found via the established orders of the religious life or in the clerical state.

More typically, however, saints came from the educated classes with an over-representation of those who were from the clerical or religious ranks or the aristocracy. Dante's *Paradiso* is peopled by such saints who not only serve as such models but also typify the heavenly circles that Dante is visiting. Such emblematic figures also afford the poet opportunity to issue prophetic judgments on those who were the anti-types of the virtues that the saints possessed. Thus, to cite an example, Saint Peter excoriates the pope who was the protector of his own tomb in Rome: "My place [i.e. Saint Peter's in Rome] which in the sight of God is empty / has made of my tomb a sewer of blood and filth / so that the

Perverse One [Satan] who fell from here above now takes comfort there below" (*Paradiso* xxvii. 23–7).

Students of medieval saints have noted that men were far more likely to be canonized while, frequently, the women who were canonized came from the aristocratic classes if they were not foundresses or conspicuous mystics. The most prominent shift happened after the twelfth century when saints were more frequently found in urban settings. For women, urban life gave them more support for their lives and, as frequently happened, there was a certain civic pride in having a "living saint."

The churches of the East have been particularly creative in classifying saints less by their station in life and more by the particular gospel values that they exemplify. The Slavic tradition honors those who live ascetic lives in the wilderness (Russian *Pustiniky*) like the great hermit and monastic founder Saint Sergius of Radonezh (died 1392), who is honored both in the East and the West, or the fifth-century Syrian monk Saint Alexander, who is numbered among the "Sleepless Ones" (Greek: *akimetes*) for his practice of constant prayer. We noted above that the Byzantine liturgy honors the "moneyless ones" (Greek: *anargyroi*) like the brothers Cosmas and Damien who offered their medical skill to the poor without charge. The Russian Church honors the two eleventh-century brothers Boris and Gleb under the beautiful title of "Passion Bearers" because they died willingly rather than being the occasion for more violence. They refused to take up arms against their older brother to dispute the right to inherit their father's title. By such a refusal they avoided the outbreak of civil war with all the violence that entailed. These "Passion Bearers" are pacifist martyrs. It is interesting that Pope Benedict XIII approved their cult as martyrs in the Roman Catholic Church in 1724. Their names now appear in the Roman martyrology for July 24. Finally, from the days of the early desert dwellers until well into the nineteenth century, both the Greek and Russian Churches have honored "Fools for Christ" – poor, eccentric, often despised wanderers who secretly carried within them a burning love for Christ, who willingly accepted the gibes of the world and the humiliations that went with them.[8] Such fools were free to speak truth to power so, not infrequently, they served a prophetic function much like the court jesters in Western monarchical systems.

Pilgrimage

Geoffrey Chaucer famously begins his *Canterbury Tales* as a group of people set out on pilgrimage from London to Canterbury to visit the blessed martyr's shrine of Saint Thomas Becket: "They come, the holy blessed martyr there to seek / who gave his help to them when they were sick." Among those travelers is the Wife of Bath who is an indefatigable pilgrim. The prologue lists her destinations: "She had been thrice to Jerusalem / had wandered over many a foreign stream / and she had been at Rome, and at Boulogne / Saint James of Compostella and Cologne . . ."

The urge to go to see the sites associated with the life of Christ in the Holy Land (our English word "saunter" comes from "*a saint terre*" to go to the Holy Land), or to visit the ascetics in the deserts of the Middle East, had been a staple of the period after the persecutions. By the Middle Ages vast numbers of people, both clerical and lay, trod the traditional pilgrimage roads to visit the tombs of the apostles in Rome or the shrine of Saint James at Compostela in Spain (still a favorite pilgrimage trip) or to venerate the Virgin of Chartres or the burial place of the Three Magi in Cologne's cathedral. More modest destinations were available to everyone in Europe. Local pilgrimages were a staple of medieval society. Modern demographic studies have estimated that there were nearly fifteen hundred datable shrine locations in Western Europe around 1400, which does not even account for minor holy places which were the objects of visits.[9]

The shrine of Saint James the Apostle at Compostela is interesting not only because it is still a favorite of pilgrims but also because of the origins of the cult. There is a ninth-century reference to relics of Saint James being transferred from Jerusalem to Spain. Through royal patronage the cult of the saint and his relics moved to Compostela where there was already a shrine to early martyrs. Because of the enormous popularity of the pilgrimage the iconography of the saint made him a fellow pilgrim with his pilgrim's hat and a cockle shell, which was the badge of those who made the pilgrimage, just as the palm branch was the badge of those who made the pilgrimage to Jerusalem (hence the surname Palmer).

Why did pilgrims travel? The reasons were various. Some were sent on pilgrimage as an act of penance, while others took to the pilgrimage road for the same reason but on their own initiative. Celtic monks went on perpetual pilgrimage (self-exile) as an ascetical practice. Others went in fulfillment of a vow to make a pilgrimage as a thanksgiving for a favor received through the intercession of a saint. Many went on pilgrimage for the same reason that people prayed to the saints in their own locales: to seek a favor or to pray for a cure from an illness. Chaucer mentions at the beginning of *The Canterbury Tales* that his pilgrims traveled both to thank and to petition for cures at the shrine of the martyr. Still others traveled as a penitential way of life or to visit a shrine in order to discern how they were to live in the future.

The popularity of pilgrimage has not diminished over the centuries. The contemporary mania for travel holidays still contains a significant element of the pilgrimage in it. Christians still travel to the Holy Land (the famous travel service of Thomas Cook & Sons began as a nineteenth-century service for those going to the Holy Land), to the shrines of Lourdes and Fatima, to Compostela or to Chartres on walking pilgrimages, and to the city of Rome. The vast throngs who visit Rome during the jubilee years are part of a tradition that goes back to the proclamation of the first Holy Year by Pope Boniface VIII in 1300.

Pilgrimage is so deeply embedded in the Christian imagination that it has become a metaphor for the Christian life itself.

The metaphor is reflected in everything from John Bunyan's seventeenth-century allegorical book *The Pilgrim's Progress* to the Second Vatican Council's adaptation of the metaphor "The Pilgrim People of God" as a description of the nature of the church itself. One can think of the medieval masterpiece, Dante's *Divinia Commedia*, as a vast metaphorical description of the Christian life itself as a journey from sin (hell) through purification (purgatory) into union with God (paradise). Indeed, the poet himself reaches for the pilgrimage motif to describe the end of his journey, dazzled by the ranks of the saints, before he has had a momentary glimpse of the "still point of light" which stands for the vision of God: "And like a pilgrim resting in the church of his vow as he looks around and hopes some day to tell of it again / so, making my way through the living light / I carried my eyes through the ranks, up and down, and now looking around again . . ." (*Paradiso* xxxi. 43–8).

Venerating Saints: A Theological Clarification

It has been argued – and the argument would take on a more pointed thrust in the Protestant Reformation – that the veneration of the saints not only detracted from the sole worship of God but, in the popular mind, could actually foster a kind of polytheism. We have seen that, as early as Augustine's treatise on *The City of God*, this complaint had been addressed.

What was the distinction between the veneration of the saints and the worship of God? The issue was clarified in the Christian East during the eighth and ninth centuries during the controversy known as iconoclasm. A strong reaction against the use of painted images of Christ, Mary, the angels, and the saints erupted in the world of Byzantium. Icons were destroyed in many places and users of icons were punished and even executed. The reasons for this iconoclastic outbreak have been debated, but many influences may be alleged: iconoclasm was a final reaction against paganism; there was the absolute prohibition of images clearly stated in the Old Testament; and, finally, there may have been influences coming from the rise of Islam and its total rejection of any kind of pictorial art.

Supporters of the use of icons in piety (the so-called "iconodules" or "image venerators") were forced to make some careful distinctions in order to resist the logic of the iconoclasts. At the most elementary level, they made a distinction between an idol (Greek: *eidolon*) and an image (Greek: *eikon*). The former was worshiped in the pagan world, while the latter was only venerated as a vehicle to go beyond the image to the reality behind it. The defenders of icons did not at all defend the worship of idols.

Second, and more importantly, the defenders of the use of icons distinguished the veneration of icons as sacred or holy objects from the worship of the person(s) depicted. They then further distinguished the absolute worship of God from the veneration due the saints. The greatest of the defenders of the use of icons was Saint John of Damascus (*c.*655–750) who wrote three treatises between 726 and 730 defending the use of icons. From his writings we have a set of crucial distinctions which may be summarized as follows: we honor (Greek: *time*) sacred images, we venerate (Greek: *proskynesis*) those who are depicted in the images, but we worship (Greek: *latreia*) God alone.[10]

The iconoclastic controversy was so heated and divisive in the Byzantine world that in order to settle the controversy an ecumenical council was convened in 787 at Nicaea. This Second Council of Nicaea was the last one held by the undivided churches of the East and West. The conciliar documents affirmed the legitimacy of painted representations because they reminded people of the truths of the Bible (i.e. they had a pedagogical value) and inspired people to greater piety, while reminding people that such persons as those depicted were not mythical or fictive but real personages who lived and live. The decree then adds: "Indeed, the honor paid to an image traverses it, reaching the model and the one who venerates the image, venerates the person represented in that image."

Even though the Council did not definitively settle the iconoclastic controversy, it did mark the beginning of the end for the image-breakers' movement. The decision in favor of the legitimacy of icons was crucial for the Byzantine Church since the place of icons in its practice is one of its signal characteristics. It is a mark of the importance of that event that to this day the Byzantine calendar celebrates annually the feast called "The Triumph of Orthodoxy" to commemorate the decision made in Nicaea in 787.

The distinctions developed in response to iconoclasm have a wider application with respect to the invocation of the saints more generally. They are intercessors before God (we join their prayers with ours), models to be emulated, and teachers of the faith by their virtues. That role is clearly indicated in the liturgy of the Christian church. One sees this by a simple examination of the prayers stipulated for saints' days. The collect prayer of the Latin rite for the feast of Saint John of Damascus on his feast day (December 4 in both the Roman Catholic and Orthodox Churches) makes the point clearly: "Lord, may the prayers of Saint John of Damascus help us / and may the true faith he taught so well be our light and our strength. We ask this *through* Our Lord Jesus Christ, your Son / who lives and reigns with You and the Holy Spirit, One God / for ever and ever. Amen" (emphasis added).

Chapter 3

Reformations: Protestant and Catholic

Greet every saint in Christ Jesus.

Philippians 4: 21

The Age of the Reformers

Although the papacy claimed jurisdiction over all canonizations and the authentication of saints' relics in the thirteenth century, it has been estimated by reliable scholars that only about ten percent of the saints venerated in the Western church were those who had been raised to the altar by papal decree. Those saints who had been venerated "from time immemorial" were still very much the objects of devotion. There were no retro-active acts of canonization. Many of those saints are central figures in the liturgical and theological life of the church, like the saints invoked in the Eucharistic canon of the Roman liturgy. Their liturgical recognition functioned in its own way as a form of informal canonization. This ancient tradition of honoring the saints, their burial places, and their relics, of course, deeply em-bedded in the popular piety and the liturgical life of the church, was also open to abuse.

Dissatisfaction with the abuses and excesses associated with the cult of the saints, their relics, and pilgrimages to their shrines, it is clear, was not a product of the Protestant Reformation. As early as 1215 the Fourth Lateran Council, one of a series of reforming councils held in Rome's Lateran Cathedral, had to intervene about the abuses connected to the selling of relics or showing them by alms collectors without proper documentation. That such a cry for reform was not an idle one is clear from the description of the Pardoner, in the prologue of Chaucer's *Canterbury Tales*, whose knapsack contained, among other things, "a brass cross set with pebble stones and a glass reliquary of pig's bones" which he would use to gull country priests with his "double talk and tricks." Chaucer was writing three generations after the Fourth Lateran Council had ended. While Chaucer derided the excesses attached to relics, his near contemporaries (for example, the Lollards) were active in calling the whole issue of the cult of the saints into question. Indeed, abuses connected to the (mis)use of relics was so common in medieval literature that it would be otiose to cite specific instances.

Voices in the late medieval church also raised their objections to the too easy slide from veneration into superstition, the spurious multiplication of relics and trafficking in them, and the degeneration of healing into forms of popular magic. One hears Thomas à Kempis in *The Imitation of Christ* chiding those who love to go on pilgrimage but find little satisfaction in a quiet cell meditating on the Word of God. Respected scholars like the fifteenth-century theologian and spiritual writer John Gerson, known as the "Most Christian Doctor" (*Doctor Christianissimus*), and his older contemporary Cardinal Nicholas of Cusa, inveighed against such abuses. Erasmus of Rotterdam, as we have noted, turned his vitriolic pen against the cult of the saints in works like *The Praise of Folly*. What Erasmus most objected to was the reduction of the cult of the saints into a superstitious tic so that "if anyone addresses a statue of Saint Barbara in the set formula he will return from battle unhurt . . . in [Saint] George they found another Hercules. They piously deck out his horse with trappings and amulets and practically worship it . . ." He concludes his diatribe: "The saint will protect you if you will try to imitate his life – if, I repeat, your wise man starts blurting out these uncomfortable truths, you can see how he will soon destroy the world's peace of mind and plunge it into confusion!"

What was seen by such critics was the vast rift between a devotion that was object centered (on this relic or that shrine) and any sense of going beyond the object. It was precisely the loss of this "going beyond" that made it possible for devotion to slide easily into a form of magic. The same critics realized that the deeper truths of the Christian faith were compromised as credulous people manipulated objects as objects. Excesses concerning the cult of relics, in effect, had mechanized religion. In other words, excesses derived from the veneration of the saints and their relics detached such practices from the mainstream of the Christian faith, creating, for some, a parallel form of degraded religion deracinated from the central claims of Christianity.

Both Thomas à Kempis and Erasmus had been influenced by that late medieval spiritual movement which has become known as *Devotio Moderna*. Beginning in the Low Countries at the end of the fourteenth century and spreading slowly into parts of Germany, France, and Italy, the promoters of the "new devotion" put a strong emphasis on the cultivation of the interior life through disciplined meditation. Strongly influenced by the christology coming from Cistercian and Franciscan antecedents, the movement had a fundamental orientation towards virtue, separation from the world, the imitation of Christ, and interior piety. While the devotees of the "new devotion" were perfectly orthodox Catholics, they tended to react against public and exterior displays of piety in favor of a more interiorized religion and an emphasis on moral improvement. As one of the scholars who knows this tradition well remarked, their spirit of renewal was an alternative to the "perfunctory practice" by which holy days became holidays, pilgrimages became tourism, and so on.[1]

Be that as it may, it is also a safe generalization to say that in the late Middle Ages every village and town in Christian Europe had its church dedicated to a saint. The cult of the saints could veer off into superstition, but the place of the saints in the practice of Christianity was firmly in place. If a religious order had a foundation in that town there was also a church under its aegis with its own favorite saint. The annual patronal feast day was an occasion of festive solemnity. Children were named for saints. Shrines and pictures dotted the walls on public thoroughfares. Confraternities, sodalities, and guilds, if they existed, had their patrons and, further, their own feast-day commemorations. Visitors to towns, villages, and cities in traditional Catholic countries today will see empirical evidence of how closely woven the cult of the saints was in the life of the town and the parishes within that town. Eamon Duffy's now classic study of popular religion in England in the fifteenth and sixteenth centuries gives vivid testimony to this fact.[2]

Martin Luther, very much a person of his age, was not totally antagonistic to the veneration of the saints. He himself cried out to Saint Anne (the patroness of miners) in his youth at a moment of distress when he was nearly killed by a stroke of lightning and, as a consequence, joined the Augustinians. What he did very much object to, when he broke with the Roman Church, was the detachment of the cult of the saints from its moorings in the saving mysteries of Christ. It was clear to him that too often the veneration of the saints had turned into a worship of semi-divinities who were addressed exclusively for this or that need with no reference to Christ himself. He further objected to the cult of relics as an engine to raise monies or "sell indulgences." Only one year after posting his famous ninety-five theses on the door of the collegiate church in Wittenberg (1517) he would excoriate Frederick the Wise for his vaunted collection of relics (of which the elector was very proud) housed in the same castle church of Wittenberg. By 1523, when his break with Rome was already a fact, he would sarcastically call that church the "Church of All saints or, rather, the Church of All Devils." For Luther, the saints were those who were already in union with God in heaven as well as those who, bound through faith in Christ, were destined for that blessedness. In short, Luther imagined the saints – in the words of the creeds – as a "communion of saints" and not as some sort of sublunary pantheon.

Luther was a conservative reformer who still had deep roots in the piety and theology of the medieval and patristic eras. He gave space in his theology for some traditional saints, even though he rejected the use of relics and had little patience for pilgrimages. In a sense, Luther interiorized pilgrimage. He wanted people to travel spiritually to the Word of God and visit the prophets and evangelists rather than to Rome (where he himself as a young friar had traveled) or to Compostela in Spain. In other words, Luther turned pilgrimage into a metaphor for the cultivation of the Christian life of faith.

The most succinct reaction of Martin Luther in his claims against the Catholic cult of the saints may be found in his *Smalcald Articles* (1538). Luther affirms that the saints on earth and perhaps the saints in heaven pray for us as does Christ himself, but "it does not follow that we should invoke angels and saints, pray to them, keep fasts and festivals for them, say masses and offer sacrifices to them, establish churches, altars, and services for them, serve them in still other ways, regard them as helpers in time of need, assigning to them special functions, as the papists teach and practice. This is idolatry. Such honor belongs to God alone."

The critical reference to "helpers in time of need" may refer specifically to a widespread devotion in Northern Europe to the so-called "Fourteen Holy Helpers." These so-called "auxiliary" (i.e. helping) saints were called on for special needs since their aid was thought to be especially efficacious when invoked. Saint Barbara was invoked against lightning; Saint Antony was thought to cure ergotism and shingles (also known as "Saint Antony's fire"); Saint Erasmus, for example, was patron of sailors and protector in times of storm (the lights appearing around a ship's mast were known as "Saint Elmo's fire"); Saint Blaise protected against throat diseases (throats are still blessed on his feast day in many Catholic churches); Saint Christopher was the patron of travelers. Many superstitious practices involving these figures (some of whom were semi-legendary or of purely fictive origin) were the subject of much polemical warning and/or ridicule in the late medieval period. It was thought, for example, that if one saw the image of Saint Christopher on a given day, the viewer would not die on that day or that the invocation of a given saint would insure happy childbirth.

If Luther kept one foot in the tradition of medieval piety, other sixteenth-century reformers – John Calvin, Ulrich Zwingli, and others – looked less benignly on the cult of the saints. In their estimation, images, relics, shrines, and the devotion attached to them smacked of superstition at best and idolatry at worst. Because they explicitly rejected the doctrine of indulgences in particular, and the doctrine of purgatory more generally, they tended to see devotion to saints and their relics as part of that whole (and, in their view, heretical) scheme which, further, had no warrant in Scripture.

They, and especially their followers, not only rejected the cult of the saints but also attempted to eradicate signs of it by the wholesale abandonment of such shrines and the extirpation of images of the saints in their churches. The reaction to the devotion of the saints from many wings of the Reformation was iconoclasm pure and simple and it was not unconnected to their resistance to other Catholic doctrines. This wholesale destruction of images, paintings, and stained-glass windows was sometimes carried out illegally by rioting crowds and sometimes under the protection or encouragement of the civil authority.

Based on a reading of Old Testament texts (for example, Exodus 20: 4–6, Leviticus 5: 8–10), the destruction of images extended to figures depicting Christ, the Blessed Virgin, and, of course, the saints. What pictorial art they permitted usually took the form of woodcuts in books to illustrate the text of Scripture. The Protestant adoption of the symbol of the cross (as opposed to the Catholic crucifix with a figure attached to the cross) is a mute but telling reminder of this iconoclastic tradition unleashed by the sixteenth-century Reformation. The aniconic impulse in the Reformation was both a protest against the mediatorial role of the saints and a resistance to the potential for idolatry. It was also a clean break – even though the break varied by degrees – with the old unreformed Church of Rome. The cult of the saints was seen as unnecessary for the Christian life; indeed, it was judged a survival from a pagan past. It was common enough in polemical literature to link the devotion of the saints to pagan myths, pointing, for example, to the devotion of Saints Cosmas and Damien as a holdover from the myths of Castor and Pollux or to Saint Christopher as a thinly disguised Hercules.

The dismantling of the whole apparatus of the cult of the saints – icons, relics, feast days, intercessory prayers, pilgrimages, shrines, and so on – was an attempt to purify the new evangelical faith and, in the process, erase a whole complex of practices that seemed to be at variance with a strict reading of biblical faith. Although it was not an explicit desire, implicitly the abolition of the cult of the saints (a cult that had some links to the doctrines of indulgences, purgatory, and so on) was a gesture towards a simpler, less complicated form of Christian life. That drive for greater simplicity was mirrored in the "new" architecture of seventeenth-century reformed churches with their rejection of stained glass, their focus on the pulpit, the diminished place for the altar, and their spare walls so often depicted in Dutch genre paintings of the time. As Article 22 of the sixteenth-century Anglican Articles phrased it succinctly, such "Romish doctrine" is "a fond thing, vainly invented, and grounded upon no warranty of Scripture, but rather repugnant to the Word of God."

It is not difficult to see how the Reformers resisted the cult of the saints. If everyone who is saved is a saint, made so by the free grace of God and election by God, then the classification of greater or lesser personages or special protectors or intercessors becomes otiose. What is left of the "saints" are those who in

Christian history model the ideal Christian life like the great figures of the Bible, but this paradigmatic function hardly called either for the apparatus of the cult of the saints or for shrines to visits their remains. As the Augsburg Confession (1530, written mostly by Philip Melanchthon) put it, "The memory of the saints may be set before us, that we may follow their faith and good works . . ." (Article no. 21), but the same Confession goes on to add that "Scripture teaches not the invocation of the saints . . ." The Second Helvitic Confession, written by Henry Bullinger in 1566, asserted the matter boldly: "Saints are not to be worshiped, adored, or invoked. They are to be loved as brethren but not singularly honored; and the ancient fathers sufficiently honored the saints when they were decently buried."[3]

The Catholic Reformation

For every momentous action in history there is an inevitable reaction. The Catholic reaction to the Protestant Reformation found its most official voice in the convening of a General Council of the Church which met in the city of Trent (with a few sessions in other cities) in Northern Italy in a number of sittings that began in 1545 but did not finally finish until 1563. Its deliberations and ordinances were so influential that scholars have frequently described the period of the modern history of the Catholic Church by the adjective "Tridentine," a neologism developed from the Latin word for Trent.

It was in the twenty-fifth and final session of the Council of Trent (December 3–4, 1563) that the assembled bishops took up the matter of the veneration of the saints. They stipulated the traditional teaching of the church on this subject, directing the bishops of the Catholic world "to instruct the faithful carefully about the intercession of the saints, invocation of them, reverence for their relics, and the legitimate uses of images of them." They further took pains "to root out utterly any abuses that may have crept into these holy and saving practices, so that no representations of false doctrines should be set up which gave dangerous error to the unlettered." Reflecting bad practices of which they were undoubtedly aware, they went on to warn that all "superstition must be removed from invocation of the saints, veneration of relics, and use of sacred images; all aiming at base profit must be eliminated, etc." Bishops were further instructed that the feast days of the saints were not to degenerate into drunken feasting (saints' days were frequently also civic holidays with no manual work done on that day) and that no new relics were to be exposed or miracles to be reported without the bishop examining and then approving them.

A year after the Council closed in 1563, Pope Pius IV issued a profession of faith (November, 1564) which every bishop and candidate for a clerical benefice had to make publicly before assumption of office and every convert to Roman Catholicism had to make at the time of reception into the church. This solemn declaration was to be made in the name of God and "these holy gospels" (i.e. sworn with a hand on the Bible). Its declarations included the following: "that the saints are to be venerated and invoked; that they offer prayers to God for us and that their relics are to be venerated. I firmly assert that the images of Christ and the ever-Virgin Mother of God, as also those of the other saints, are to be kept and retained, and that due honor and veneration is to be paid to them."[4]

The Council of Trent, then, did two things. First, it reiterated the traditional teaching of the Catholic Church on the legitimacy of the invocation of the saints, the veneration of their relics, and the proper use of images within the context of Catholic worship and devotion. Second, it issued some practical instructions for bishops to check abuses in the cult of the saints and for the proper ways of fostering correct devotion. The first point affirmed traditional Catholic teaching, while the second point implicitly acknowledged past abuses and argued for vigilance against their repetition.

The Council of Trent represents the attitude of the Catholic Church in its juridical understanding. The Catholic Reformation also understood that the recognition of saints by canonization served as a strong instrument of evangelization by emphasizing that within the church there existed the means by which people reached the heights of holiness. Saints could serve as paradigmatic types, indicating how the holiness of the church was realized in the lives and doctrines of its best members.

Scholars have long noted that once canonization became formalized there was a certain sociological profile of who got canonized. Men outpaced women by a margin of four to one. Women who were canonized were either high-born aristocrats or religious superiors (or both). Men, by and large, came from the ranks of either the established (Benedictine) or emerging religious orders. Few lay persons were canonized and those who were, typically, did not come from the lower classes of society. Enough careful research has been done to demonstrate empirically the generalizations just made.[5] The point to remember is that every canonization is a sociological, theological, and political statement. The process says, in effect: here is one whom we admire and hold up as a model.

The Catholic Church, after the Reformation, used the canonization process as one instrument of its general program of reform. A thumbnail example of the kind of saint the Catholic Reformation most revered may be seen in the 1622 ceremony when Pope Gregory XV (now reposing in an elaborate tomb in St Peter's Basilica designed by Bernini) solemnly canonized five saints, including: Saint Ignatius of Loyola (1491–1556), who was the founder of the Jesuits, a militant religious order often identified as the spearhead of the Catholic Reformation; Saint Francis Xavier (1506–1552), who had been a companion of Ignatius and a missionary in the Far East; Saint Philip Neri (1515–1595), who was a model priest, born in Florence, who exercised his entire ministry in Rome and around whom the Oratorian Society of priests was founded; and Saint Teresa of Avila (1515–1582), the

Plate 3 Saint Francis Xavier (1506–1551). Museo Casa de Murillo, La Paz.
Photo Gilles Mermet / AKG-Images.

great Spanish contemplative whose religious sisters would establish in France convents that had a tremendous impact on French
spirituality in the seventeenth century.

All of these figures had lived through the tumultuous period
of the sixteenth century and all were known less for their miracles
and more for their powerful spiritual life and their Catholic zeal
for reform and evangelization. Two were founders of religious
orders (Ignatius and Philip), while a third was a reformer of an

existing order (Teresa) and a fourth (Francis Xavier) was a zealous and successful foreign missionary. The founding of reforming religious orders was, of course, one of the main instruments of the Catholic reform. Major European cities would establish in their centers large churches staffed by reforming orders like the Theatines, Capuchins, Jesuits, and Oratorians during the seventeenth century. These churches, lavishly decorated in the Baroque style, and the schools often annexed to them, would be instruments of reform and evangelization.

The beau idéal of a saint in the Catholic Reformation would be a figure like the Jesuit Peter Canisius (1521–1597). After his theological studies and his formation in the Jesuits, he worked mainly in Bavaria (but also in Vienna and Prague) where he was a zealous preacher for Catholic reform and a powerful polemicist against the Reformers. He composed an influential catechism called the Great Catechism (*Catechismus Major*), written in a question and answer format (Luther had published such a catechism using the same style), which went through many editions and remained a basic teaching instrument well into modern times. Many scholars have seen Peter Canisius as the single most powerful influence in the success of the Catholic Reformation in southern Germany.

Like Peter Canisius, Robert Bellarmine (1542–1621) was a Jesuit who, after his Jesuit formation in Italy, taught in Louvain (Belgium) and then took the chair of "controversial theology" at the Roman College. He was the most prominent apologist of his day whose three-volume defense of the Roman Catholic faith (*Disputationes de Controversiis*) was the standard response to Protestants in his time. A staunch defender of the papacy, the author of a vernacular catechism, and a biblical critic, Bellarmine's life was shaped by the struggles of the period. Both Bellarmine and Canisius would later be named "Doctors of the Church."

The fifth saint canonized by Pope Gregory XV in the 1622 ceremony was a humble Spanish lay person and peasant named Isidore the Farmer, who had lived in the Middle Ages (died 1130) and had been locally venerated in Spain for centuries. It was said that when he was lost in prayer in the fields people would see angels plowing in his stead. He was notable for his patience in the face of the jealousy of other laborers. He was canonized through the influence of Philip III of Spain, who credited the saint with his own recovery from a deadly illness. Isidore was a throwback to an earlier kind of saintliness (and a rare humble lay person from the Middle Ages to be canonized) and, in that capacity, demonstrates a contrast with his saintly companions who were very much in the mode of the Counter-Reformation saint. By juxtaposing an Isidore with an Ignatius of Loyola, however, one sees both the continuity and the newness of the hagiographical tradition. It also says something about the power of politics in such decisions.

Isidore, however, is the exception that proves the rule. The ideal candidate for sainthood in the militant church of the Catholic Reformation was either the successful apologist for Catholicism, like the Jesuit scholar Robert Bellarmine, or a reforming bishop, like Charles Borromeo, or a founder/foundress of a new religious order who carried forward the work of the Tridentine reforms. While a certain nod was given to the miraculous, increasingly saints were put forward who exemplified the ideals of the Catholic Reformation. This change in "style" also points to a homely truth: namely, that the decision about the kind of saint to be canonized is, at the same time, an apologetic and sociological decision. Canonizations send a message.

To say that the Catholic Reformation exalted a "new" kind of saint is not to say that there was a discontinuity with the older tradition of the saints. Ignatius of Loyola marked his own conversion as coming from a time in his life when he was convalescing from war wounds suffered in 1521. He read a medieval life of Christ and a Spanish translation of Jacobus de Voragine's *Golden Legend*. It was from the inspiration he gained from that period of reading that his desire for the life of God grew. It is also worth noting that in his conversion process he first attempted

Plate 4 The colonnaded arcade around St Peter's Square, Rome. Photo © John and Lisa Merrill / CORBIS.

to model his life on the lives of the saints by undertaking a series of experiments in his own life as a pilgrim, penitent, ascetic, and so on, until his life took definitive shape. When, in the famous section of Ignatius's "Rules for Thinking with the Church" in his *Spiritual Exercises*, he insists that "we should show our esteem for the relics of the saints by venerating them and praying to the saints" and "praise visits to the Station churches, pilgrimages, indulgences, jubilees, crusades, indults, and the lighting of candles in churches," this was not merely paying lip service to the sixteenth-century church but a reflection of experiences and usages that shaped his own life. Indeed, these "Rules" could make a fair claim to be the vade mecum of militant Catholicism.[6]

One strikingly visible sign of how the Catholic Reformation situated the saints may be seen in the piazza of Saint Peter's Basilica in Rome. When Bernini designed the piazza with its huge arc of colonnaded walls in the shape of an open circle, he placed over the colonnade massive statues of the saints carved in travertine. Symbolically, the saints beckoned forward the pilgrims and Roman faithful into the basilica, which was the seat of papal power and where many canonizations took place. The full ensemble of the open-air space in front of the basilica made a powerful metaphorical statement: this is the church of the saints who collectively invite you in to the altar of Peter whose body lies under the main altar.

The Reformation period was a time of great religious zeal but, as often happens, it was also the age of intense religious violence. In England, for example, when Henry VIII decreed that he was the "Supreme head on earth of the Church in England," to affirm otherwise was construed as an act of treason and punished, accordingly, by death. Nor is it surprising that Henry demolished the shrine of Thomas Becket in 1538 since it would hardly do to have a shrine dedicated to a churchman with the authority of the pope who died as a martyr at the hands of the king's nobles. Later regal decrees in the British Isles fairly equated adherence to the Catholic Church with a capital crime, decrees made all the more stern when popes released Catholics from their allegiance to the Crown. Persecution of Catholics would extend well into the seventeenth century. Even though most of those who died on the scaffold were not formally canonized until the late nineteenth and early twentieth centuries, as early as the late sixteenth century Pope Gregory XIII (died 1585) allowed the English College in Rome to have painted frescos of English martyrs with the implied idea that those who suffered during the Reformation would also find their place among the canonized.

Beginning with Sir Thomas More and extending through the sixteenth century, Catholics went to the scaffold in large numbers. Priests, who were forbidden to live in England, would enter the country in disguise to minister to Catholics. The English Catholic Church was profoundly shaped by the stories of the martyrs who risked all for the old faith. Robert Southwell (1561–1595) was one of the more famous of these English martyrs. A Jesuit poet (whose work is now part of the English canon of poetry), Southwell ministered in England from 1586 until his capture in 1592. Imprisoned in the Tower of London for nearly three years, he was already famous for his prose works (circulated in manuscript), such as "An Epistle of Comfort" which was an appeal to Catholics to remain hopeful during persecution. His poems were published soon after his death and were notable both for their deep religious feeling and their use of the literary conceits so loved by the Elizabethans.

Of course, during the reign of Queen Mary those who adhered to the Church of England also died for their religious convictions as did numbers of Anabaptists all through the century. On the continent, people died both for the Catholic and the Reformed faith. It is often difficult to distinguish those who suffered as a result of political policies reflected in the various wars of religion or to understand to what degree those who were turned over to the secular arm by the Inquisition were so condemned by reason of their faith or for reasons of state. However one understands these extremely complex issues, it is very clear that the reforming impulses, on both sides of the dispute, could count among their number many who went to their deaths for their convictions. The Anabaptists, for example, were the object of vilification and persecution both by mainstream reformers like Luther, Calvin, and Zwingli, as well as by Roman Catholics. It is estimated that those who died for their faith numbered in the tens of thousands in the sixteenth century. They left behind witness to their faith in their hymns and their martyrdom narratives. Indeed, the Anabaptist tradition holds up to this day those persons who died as witnesses for Christ.[7]

Since the Protestants had no vehicle for public recognition of their martyred dead, their form of "canonization" came mainly through the use of the printed page, the collective memory of their congregations, and the preached word. Perhaps the most famous of these Protestant martyrologies was that of the Oxford-trained John Foxe (died 1587). Foxe fled to the continent on the accession of the Catholic restorationist Queen Mary ("Bloody Mary") only to return in 1559. A memoir of the persecution of Protestants, written in Latin in 1545 while he was in Strasbourg, was expanded into an English book, published in 1563 under the title *Acts and Monuments of Matters Happening in the Church*, but more familiarly known as *Foxe's Book of Martyrs*. The work,

The Burning of Cieely Ormes at Norwich.

O.Terry Sculp 2014

Publish'd as the Act directs, by H. Trapp Pater-noster-Row.

Paternoster Row.

Plate 5 A woodcut from *Foxe's Book of Martyrs* (1563). Mary Evans Picture Library.

enhanced with vivid woodcuts, went through three more expanded editions within his lifetime. It has been said that, along with the King James Version of the Bible and the Book of Common Prayer, Foxe's work gave definitive shape to England as a Protestant nation. The *Book of Martyrs*, brought to the New World by dissidents who left England, became a staple of religious reading in North America well into the eighteenth century. To this day it is cited as an example of Christian witness among certain fundamentalists who have strong anti-Catholic sentiments as part of their worldview.

The issue of martyrdom was not without its theological problems within the world of the Reformation. In October 1659, the civil authority in Boston (Massachusetts) hanged three Quakers, with a fourth going to the gallows some months later. They were considered by the world outside the Society of Friends (Quakers) as disturbers of the peace and sowers of discord. Within the Quaker community they were seen as martyrs, and the manner of their death was described in language very similar to the acts and legends of the early Christian literature on martyrdom. The martyrdom of the Quakers generated a literature not unlike that found within Anabaptist circles of the previous century since quite often adherents of the radical reform found themselves on both Catholic and Protestant scaffolds. The "official" churches saw them as anarchists; they considered themselves dying in imitation of Christ. All things being equal, the tensions can be seen in a somewhat similar light whether one is speaking of ancient martyrdom or that of the sixteenth and seventeenth centuries (or, the twentieth, as we shall see, for that matter).[8] The memoirs of such martyrs have certain commonalities with the older hagiographies written under Catholic auspices.

Catholics, of course, also canonized some martyrs who died at the hands of the Reformers (the first group of English martyrs was beatified in 1886), but they found an even richer crop of martyrs who died in the wake of the vigorous missionary expansion of the church as new orders like the Jesuits, as well as older, more established orders, sent personnel into the worlds being opened by exploration. In 1930, for example, Pope Pius XI canonized eight Jesuits who were killed by Native Americans in the New World in the seventeenth century; they are known collectively as the Martyrs of North America. Nearly forty years earlier (1893), a group of Jesuits martyred in India were beatified. The first missionaries in Indochina (Vietnam) were beatified in 1900.

The canonization of these (and other) martyrs points out another aspect of the Catholic Reformation: namely, its aggressive overseas missionary effort. This effort, outside the world of Central and Latin America where Catholic missionaries accompanied the first explorers, was a conscious effort to expand the Roman Catholic Church throughout the world. It is noteworthy that a separate Vatican congregation to oversee missionary activity was established in the early seventeenth century (1622) and, in 1627, a separate missionary college. That congregation remains in Rome to this day, but in 1988 it was renamed the Congregation for the Evangelization of Nations, and the university founded in the seventeenth century also exists.

The Papal Curia and Canonization

We have already seen that the formal canonization of saints in the Roman Catholic Church was reserved to the papacy from the time of the thirteenth century. In the wake of the Council of Trent and its desire to avoid abuses in the matter of the saints, new legislation developed as an instrument for overseeing the causes of the saints. This legislative urge was part of the larger tendency to centralize church authority in the papal curia in order to guarantee the unity of the church and to specify, through precise legislation, the mechanism for the canonization process.

The canonization process and oversight for authenticating relics was put in the hands of the papal Congregation of Rites which had been established by Pope Sixtus V in 1588. That office provided a practical way of enforcing the will of the Council of Trent. In 1634 Pope Urban VIII established detailed rules for beatifications (i.e. for those who might enjoy a local cult) and canonizations (for those who would be enrolled in the universal calendar of the saints) with the further stipulation that no person might be venerated or their writings published without prior scrutiny and authorization by Rome. Any attempt to contravene that regulation disqualified a person from consideration. That stern stipulation was put in place to gain some control over errant ecstatics, visionaries, and others who might have generated a local cult following. The only exception to this general rule was for those who had been venerated from "time immemorial." which means, as we have seen, those who were already venerated in the church before formal canonization processes were in place.

The Congregation of Rites worked within the framework of this legislation until the eighteenth century. Between 1734 and 1738 the noted canonist and scholar Prospero Lambertini (later Pope Benedict XIV), who worked in the Congregation of Rites as a canon lawyer, published a multi-volume work under the title *On the Beatification of the Servants of God and the Canonization of the Blessed* which became the standard work on canonization until well into the twentieth century. The procedures outlined in that work were later condensed into the church's canon law and were not modified until 1983 when Pope John Paul II issued an apostolic constitution under the title *Divinus Perfectionis Magister* ("The Divine Teacher of Perfection") which is the set of vastly simplified procedures used today.

The process outlined by Lambertini was a complex one. Petitions for beatification were initiated at a local level under the care of the bishop. Except in the case of martyrdom, this process could only begin fifty years after the person's death. A completed dossier was forwarded to Rome where it was assigned an advocate called a *postulator* whose advocacy was critiqued by the Defender of the Faith (known familiarly as the "Devil's Advocate"). When this process was completed, a formal dossier (known as the *positio*) was presented to the Congregation who began a more formal process after receiving the approval of the pope. In most cases, if circumstances warranted, the body of the person was exhumed since an uncorrupted body was considered a sign of great sanctity. For the case of beatification to proceed, two well-attested miracles through the intercession of the person were demanded – with the examination of the miracles also contested by the Defender of the Faith. After beatification, there was the requirement of a further two miracles for canonization. The pope only presided at the canonization mass; for beatification, he merely venerated the person after the beatification ceremonies. Almost without exception these rites were performed in Saint Peter's Basilica in Rome.[9] This cumbersome set of steps almost guaranteed that the procedure of canonization was a slow one with some cases languishing for decades (and even centuries) in the canonical process. Some cases have never been resolved. Thomas à Kempis, for example, the fifteenth-century author of *The Imitation of Christ*, has long been thought of as a saint but his cause has, up till now, never gone forward. The reforms initiated by Pope John Paul II, as we shall see, accelerated beatifications and canonizations to what, from the Roman perspective, was almost warp speed.

These procedures may seem overly legal, but the very process articulated by the Catholic Church inevitably demanded some respect for historical verisimilitude in making the case for canonization. The development of the canonization process coincided with the rise of a more rigorous approach to history, which coincidence would have ramification in the history of saints.

The Saints and Scholarship

The martyrology in use in the Roman Church in the sixteenth century was a swollen compilation of the old list of the Roman martyrs to which numerous additions from Africa, Greater Syria, and other canons of saints had been added. There were also extant various compilations done at the hands of individuals over the centuries, to say nothing of the compilations made by the various religious orders in the church. In the most recent edition of the Roman martyrology (2001) that old martyrology was succinctly described as *geminationibus, confusionibus, aliisque erroribus obscuratum* (riddled with doublets, obscurities, and other errors). Accordingly, a commission of ten learned men was established in the sixteenth century to correct the martyrology, as part of the general reform of the Roman liturgy inspired by Trent. The result of their work was published under the authority of Pope Gregory XIII in 1584. Gregory had been at the Council of Trent as a representative of the curia and was a keen supporter of reform. It was this pope who compiled the reformed corpus of canon law, began the reform of Gregorian chant, and decreed the switch to the Julian calendar by dating the day after October 4, 1582 as October 15, 1582. The 1584 Roman martyrology was still not perfect. The great church historian, Caesar Baronius (1538–1607), who had been a leading member of the original commission of ten, saw through new corrections in 1586 and 1589. Nearly two hundred years later, Pope Benedict XIV who, as Prospero Lambertini wrote the official instructions for the beatification and canonization process, again radically corrected the martyrology in 1748.

The correction of the martyrology was part of the larger project of emending and updating the liturgical books in general. The martyrology was, and still is, even today, however, little more than a daily listing of the name of a particular saint, where the saint was from, and when and how the saint died. A far more serious issue had to do with the readings of the saints' lives in the official liturgy of the church. It was the custom during the nocturns of the night office to read in the intervals between the chanting of the psalms some abbreviated life and deeds of the saint being honored on that day. That is why, as we saw in the case of Saint Francis in chapter 2, that some of the *legenda* were written in briefer form "for use in the choir" (i.e. in the liturgical service). The readings in the second nocturn were often piously edifying but historically suspect, giving rise to the old Roman clerical gibe directed at those who trimmed the truth: "You lie like a second nocturn!"

In the period of the Renaissance and the Reformation there was a keen interest, thanks to the rise of humanist education, in history. History could serve, among other things, as a polemical tool in the religious wars and as an instrument of internal church reform. Historical research and philological analysis were by no means an invention of the Renaissance. Abelard brought down wrath on his head when he argued, in the early twelfth century, that the patron of his abbey of Saint Denis could not be the Dionysius the Areopagite converted by Paul in Athens according to Acts 17. Only in the fifteenth century did the Florentine humanist Lorenzo Valla demonstrate that Dionysius, author of various important theological works, was the fictive name of a late fifth-century Syrian monk who had assumed that name under which he wrote some extremely influential works hitherto attributed to a New Testament figure. The real Saint Denis honored in Paris was a third-century Italian who was sent to Gaul and became an effective missionary in the environs of Paris. He died in the Decian persecution of 250 and the chapel built over his tomb later became the site of the Benedictine Abbey of St Denis. Somehow, this third-century martyr became conflated with Dionysius the Areopagite – a not infrequent conflation in the history of hagiography.

The Belgian Jesuit Heribert Rosweyde (died 1629) conceived a plan to write the lives of the saints based on research in original sources. He did not live to take up this work so it was left to his compatriot and fellow Jesuit, John van Bolland (died 1665) to initiate the project. Bolland and his collaborators searched for sources in the libraries of Europe in order to write the most authentic lives that their researches could produce. What they soon discovered was that the historical basis for some saints was negligible at best. They also discovered that certain traditional lives were constructed from popular romances, fevered imaginations, the blending of folktales into the narratives, and the conflation of stories based on the similarities of names. Needless to say, their researches were not always popular with either the general public or, in some cases, religious authorities. Their assertion that the Old Testament prophet Elijah was not the founder of the Carmelite order as pious members of that order believed, resulted in an ugly pamphlet war with some of their polemical work coming to the attention of the Spanish Inquisition. Rome finally acted in a fashion that was wise and ordered a stop to the dispute in perpetuity without adjudicating the case. That solomonic decision allowed the Carmelites to look back to the ascetic tradition of Mount Carmel, while the Bollandists were able to continue their scholarly researches.

Pope Benedict XIV was (not surprisingly given his own role in the development of the canonization protocols) a keen supporter of the Bollandists' efforts, so their research continued until the suppression of the Jesuits in the late eighteenth century. With the Jesuits reconstituted in 1837, the work of the Society of the Bollandists continues in Antwerp to this day. The research of the Bollandists finds its outlet in a number of scholarly publications. Its journal *Analecta Bollandiana* (founded in 1882) appears twice a year. Specialized monographs are part of a series called *Subsidia Hagiographica* which began in 1886. Their greatest work, of course, is the monumental *Acta Sanctorum*, whose first volume for the saints honored in the month of January saw light in Antwerp in 1643, but, with revisions and additions, their work on the saints continues to this day. Their work still stands in the highest regard among those who are professionally interested in hagiography.[10]

In addition, the Benedictine monks associated with the Abbey of Saint Maur, founded in France in 1618 as part of a reforming impulse in French monasticism, initiated a program of research and publication in matters theological and historical that extended into the late eighteenth century. While the work of the Maurists, as they were known, was not directly focused on matters hagiographical, they contributed indirectly to the rise of serious historical scholarship which impinged on the subject of the saints. Their far-ranging publications, produced by generations of monk scholars, provided important sources on the history of monasticism, works on asceticism, and editions of the Fathers (like their important edition of the works of Saint Augustine), which provided a serious historical matrix for a clearer and less fabulous approach to the history of the saints.

Chapter 4

Towards the Modern World

The Sea of Faith
Was once, too, at the full . . .

Matthew Arnold

Worlds Divided

One major result of the Protestant Reformation was Europe's geographical division along religious lines – lines mirrored in those places in the New World that saw colonial expansion, since the Reformation more or less coincided with the great age of European exploration. Most of what is present-day Latin and Central America became Roman Catholic; most of colonial North America was either Protestant (the colonies along the Atlantic seaboard) or Catholic (the francophone parts of Canada). Similar religious fault lines would occur with the colonial expansion into Africa and elsewhere. Well towards the end of the eighteenth century the idea of the separation of church and state was not considered as a desirable political ordering of affairs. Religious minorities at odds with the majority were at best tolerated but more frequently proscribed or suffered various kinds of civil disabilities. Therefore, the cult of the saints in areas of the world colonized by Catholics tended to mirror the home countries, while the absence of such a cult reflected the same attitude as that found in Europe.

The Byzantine world, home of orthodoxy, had been trauma-tized by the fall of Constantinople in the middle of the fifteenth century, so that, with the exception of some parts of Eastern Europe (and Russia), Christians lived under the authority of the Ottoman Empire which extended from its natural Turkish bound-aries in the Middle East as far west as Greece. Christians lived in the Middle East at the sufferance of and subject to the law of their Islamic rulers. Greece itself did not wrest its autonomy away from the Ottoman Empire until the nineteenth century.

In the traditional European Catholic countries, the cult of the saints was still a part of Catholic life. In the official liturgy of the church, in particular the mass, the feasts of the saints were observed according to the reforms set out by the Council of Trent. With the exception of the calendars of the various religious orders, the calendar of the saints was uniform. Uniformity, in fact, was both the desideratum and the reality of Roman Catholic life after Trent. One could go anywhere in the world and the Latin rite mass would be celebrated according to the same rites stipulated by the Roman missal which had been published by Pope Pius V in 1570. With some local exceptions, the calendar of saints' feast days was uniform throughout the Catholic world. That missal had a preface with details of how the rites were to be exercised, with rubrics as particular as how far apart the priest's hands were to be when saying the prayers at the altar. It is worthwhile noting that, except for those places with par-ticular liturgical rites hallowed by antiquity (for example, the Ambrosian rite in Milan or the Mozarabic in Toledo in Spain) where a different liturgical practice had been in place for at least two hundred years, this missal, with minor updating, would be the standard for the Roman rite mass right up until the liturgical reforms of the Second Vatican Council (which ended in 1965).

The Roman missal stipulated an annual calendar which was divided into two parts. The temporal cycle (called the *Temporale*) commemorated the mysteries of Christ, beginning with the four weeks before Christmas (Advent) and running through the time of Epiphany, Lent, Holy Week, and on to Pentecost with the Sundays after Pentecost leading again to the Advent season. The second cycle was that of the saints (the so-called *Sanctorale*), which marked off the days for the celebration of the feasts of those saints who were universally venerated in the church. The Roman missal of Pius V originally listed about 130 saints in this cycle who were venerated in the universal church, but over subsequent years this number would swell when people were canonized and inserted into the universal calendar of the saints, although such additions were infrequent. The only concession to diversity was permission for the long-standing custom of local churches to celebrate saints' days that had particular significance for a particular locale. Rites for these celebrations were included in appendices to the Roman missal. Particular religious orders also had the use of a sanctoral cycle within which they were able to celebrate feast days of saints peculiar to their given religious order.[1]

The sanctoral cycle was always subservient to the temporal cycle. Feast days of saints were not celebrated on Sundays and typically the Lenten season diminished the feasts of the saints except for extraordinary patronal saints days in a given locale. Regional customs would enhance certain feasts of the saints when they involved a national patron or that of a particular diocese or a town or village within a diocese. Such enhancements were left to the customs of the place. The various religious orders, as we have noted, had their own sanctoral cycles where festive ceremonies would be celebrated on their founder's day or on the occasion of some conspicuous saint who was a member of a given order. As a generalization, one could say that in the Roman Catholic Church there was a uniformity of celebration with some concessions made to local needs. Well into the twentieth century national saints' days were also civil holidays in traditionally Catholic countries.

The observance of a sanctoral cycle in the churches of the Reformation varied widely. In those churches under Lutheran influence the sanctoral cycle rapidly disappeared. In the various permutations of the early editions of the Anglican *Book of Common Prayer* the number of saints' days waxed and waned depending on whether the regnant powers were Catholic or Puritan by inspiration. The churches under the influence of Geneva simply erased the cycle of saints in fidelity to the great NO of John Calvin. Calvin thought that the intercession of the saints derived from a lack of faith in Jesus Christ as the sole mediator between humanity and God. By palliating this anxiety, Calvin wrote, "They dishonor Christ and rob him of his title as sole mediator, a title, which given him by the Father as his special privilege ought not to be transferred to another" (*Institutes of the Christian Religion* III. 20. 21).

New Forms of Religious Life

One of the most powerful instruments of Catholic reform, as we noted in chapter 3, was the renewal or foundation of religious orders. In the sixteenth century, for example, Spanish Catholicism was invigorated by the reform of the Carmelites through the work of Saint Teresa of Avila and her younger contemporary, Saint John of the Cross (1542–1591). Teresa's Carmelite reforms were doubly important because after her death her reformed convents made foundations in France and their spirituality provided the matrix out of which developed the so-called French School of Spirituality. The French School, as we shall see, gave birth to a wide variety of new religious communities. Other reforming orders would include the Jesuits, the Theatines in Italy, and the reformed branch of the Franciscans who took their names from their long hoods (*capuches*), the Capuchins.[2] What was particularly significant, however, was a profound shift in the ways in which women were being formed in the religious life.

Women have lived the monastic life from its beginnings. It was expected that women who chose such a life would be strictly cloistered and such was the case right down to the time of the Protestant Reformation. Some attempts had been made in the medieval period to model a different form of religious living for women (for example, the Beguines) but without any enthusiasm on the part of church authority. At times, some women lived as tertiaries or as independent women observing some sort of rule but these were understood as being contemplative in character. This situation would change, beginning in the sixteenth century. Saint Angela of Merici (1474–1540), for example, gathered a group of women into a small community in Brescia in 1533, who wore no habit, lived with their families, and began to teach poor children under the patronage of Saint Ursula. When Angela died in 1540 she was widely revered as a living saint (however, she was not canonized until 1807) and four years later her congregation gained official recognition as a religious community. The Ursuline Sisters, dedicated to education, prospered and continue to teach and do other apostolic works to this day.[3]

Saint Francis de Sales (1567–1622), the great reforming bishop of Geneva, theologian, and noted spiritual writer, founded in tandem with his dear friend Saint Jane de Chantal (1572–1641) the Visitation Sisters. These sisters were to care for children, the sick, and the needy in their cloistered environs. Because of resistance to the idea of non-enclosure they were unable completely to depart from the idea of the cloister, but they did attempt to modify cloistered life in order to serve those outside the convent. Saint Vincent de Paul (1581–1660) had more success in this matter. He first began to organize women's groups in many parishes around Paris to care for the poor. Since upper-class women could not do such work personally, he started a second group known as the *Filles de Charité* (Daughters of Charity) by recruiting young women from the country. He put the formation of these women in the hands of Saint Louise de Marillac (1591–1660). Out of this movement, originally a "confraternity," grew a religious congregation approved by Rome in 1668. Vincent had what – for that time – was a radical vision. As he told these sisters in words that have almost become proverbial: "For your cell, a rented room; for your chapel, the parish church; for a cloister, the streets of the city . . . Fear of God is your grill and modesty your veil." The Daughters of Charity, with their characteristic "butterfly" headdress (originally simply the clothing of Breton country women), would become famous for their service to the poor of the world.

It would take a separate volume to list and describe the many religious congregations founded by women in the modern period of Catholicism. In the United States of America, for instance, there are nearly 450 religious congregations of women. The large majority of these congregations are "active" ones (as opposed to cloistered communities) with, again, the vast majority having been founded in the late eighteenth or early nineteenth century. Suffice it to say that there are literally many more hundreds of such communities scattered over the globe. Many simply started when a small group of women banded together to do works of charity and then subsequently organized themselves under a bishop's authority into a religious congregation. The Catholic Church has beatified or canonized many such foundresses who have labored in North and South America, Europe, Africa, and Asia. Saint Julie Billiart (1751–1816) was the French-born foundress of the Sisters of Notre Dame whose members by the twentieth century were found in most parts of the world. In the United States of America, the wealthy heiress Katherine Drexel (1858–1955) founded the Sisters of the Blessed Sacrament in 1891 to work exclusively with Native Americans and African Americans, while the convert Rose Hawthorne (1851–1926), daughter of the eminent American writer Nathaniel Hawthorne, founded a religious community dedicated to the sick and dying sufferers of cancer. Mary MacKillop, Australia's first native canonized saint (in 1995), founded the Josephite Sisters in Australia who dedicated themselves to education and to the care of orphans.

The Catholic world of Latin and Central America was shaped by the impact of Iberian Catholicism. Well into the modern world mixed blood and indigenous people were reluctantly accepted into religious orders or were simply excluded from consideration. As a consequence, some of the saints from that part of the world had to be satisfied with marginal roles in church life. Martin de Porres (1579–1639), for instance, was the illegitimate son of a Spanish knight and a Panamanian woman who became a lay brother in the Dominican monastery in Lima, Peru, where he gained a powerful reputation both for his love of the poor and his penitential life. Remaining a lay brother for his entire life, he managed to found a shelter for abandoned babies and an orphanage while also working with African slaves. His friend, Rose of Lima (1586–1617), though of Spanish parentage, resisted marriage and lived as a Dominican tertiary in a garden shack. Enormously popular with the people of Lima because of her ascetic life, she was credited with forestalling an earthquake that struck the outskirts of the city. Her way of life was not unlike that of many women in Europe (for example, Catherine of Siena) who were not technically nuns but lived lives of great piety. She is the first canonized saint (in 1671) from the New World and is honored as the patroness of all of Latin America.

There was a similar, if more modest, proliferation of religious congregations of men that can also trace their origins to the reforming impulses of the modern period in the Catholic Church. Saint John of God (1495–1550) founded an order of brothers to care for the sick, and Saint Camillus de Lellis (1550–1614) founded an order for the same purpose. Pope Leo XIII named both of these founders as patron saints of the sick. Saint Vincent de Paul not only co-founded the Daughters of Charity but also a community of men known as the Congregation of the Mission (known more familiarly as the Vincentians after their founder) who evangelized the countryside in France but also, in Vincent's own lifetime, went abroad as missionaries. Saint John Baptist de La Salle (1651–1719) founded the Institute of the Brothers of the Christian Schools (known more commonly as the Christian Brothers) which became one of the largest congregations of religious brothers in the world. The so-called French School of Spirituality produced two other saints who founded religious communities: Saint John Eudes (1601–1680), who founded the Congregation of Jesus and Mary (the Eudists) after a long period in the Oratorians, and Saint Louis Mary Grignion (1673–1716), who a year before his death organized a company of priests into what would later become a congregation known as the DeMontfort Fathers.

In Italy, Saint Alphonsus Mary de Liguori (1696–1787) founded the Congregation of the Most Holy Redeemer in 1732 which was devoted to mission work in the Kingdom of Naples but which would spread, in time, into a world-wide community. His contemporary, Saint Paul of the Cross (1694–1775), founded the Discalced Clerics of the Holy Cross and the Passion – the Passionists – in 1741 dedicated, like the Redemptorists, to evangelization and the giving of missions in the Papal States.

The congregations mentioned above are representative of a flowering of communities established in the early modern period whose founders were canonized and whose efforts were oriented to the internal reform of the Catholic Church and the furthering of the works of mercy in education, health care, and outreach to the poor more generally. In addition, these congregations were keenly concerned with developing the spiritual lives of priests and working to evangelize people, especially in rural areas. What is characteristic of all of these congregations is that, in one way or another, they adapted and/or modified inherited models of the older monastic and mendicant orders in terms of the needs of the day.

It is clear that the most radical changes occurred within the congregations of women who, often against enormous clerical and hierarchical resistance, freed women for a more active and apostolic life. In this regard the story of Mary Ward (1586–1645) is a sad tale. An English woman who entered the Poor Clare Convent at Saint Omer in France in 1606, she left three years later to found a religious community of women after the model of the Jesuits. She wanted a community free from episcopal supervision answerable only to the pope, freedom from the obligation of the choral recitation of the daily office, and freedom from the restrictions of monastic enclosure. Despite some initial success, her congregation was suppressed in 1631 and she was imprisoned in a convent in Munich. Despite an appeal to the pope, she could only act on an informal basis. She returned to her native Yorkshire in 1639 and died in 1645. Only in the early eighteenth century was her Institute of the Blessed Virgin Mary approved by Rome. Mary Ward, of course, has not been canonized, but she is regarded by many as a prophetic figure and a champion of women's rights in the church.

Many of the religious communities founded in the early modern period and into our own time saw it as a mark of their zeal and service to the church that their founders and foundresses were recognized for their sanctity. As a consequence, there is a disproportionate number of religious women and men in the canon of saints. Their causes had the support, the finances, and the personnel to advance the process of canonization from the local level to the Roman one. To encourage the canonical process was natural enough since a canonized founder or foundress gave spiritual luster to the congregation in question and, implicitly, testified to the holiness of their work. Within those congregations it was only natural to seek the beatification and canonization of the founders and foundresses since such recognition put a seal of approval on the congregation's way of life, a particular spiritual charism, and provided a saintly patron (patroness) for the congregation that was so blessed.

This access to the canonical process and its eventual success, of course, led to the widespread (mistaken) general impression that only vowed religious were capable of a sanctity conspicuous enough to merit inclusion in the ranks of the canonized. It has only been in contemporary times that serious efforts have been made in the Roman Catholic Church to include lay men and women, married or single, into the ranks of the beatified and canonized. Their number, however, pales with respect to those who are in religious life – a fact that still gives some plausibility to the perception that it is in the religious life that one finds real sanctity.

Doctors of the Church

One classification of the saint which has an ancient pedigree but a somewhat different significance is that of Doctor of the Church. The concept of the title "Doctor of the Church" has a long and somewhat complicated history. The early patristic writers often spoke of the "fathers and doctors" of the church. The term "doctor" (Latin: *docere*, to teach) was used to describe the eminent teachers of doctrine in antiquity. As early as Augustine they are singled out by name, but by the time of the Venerable Bede (died 735) four names from the Western church (although there was no Eastern disagreement about the merit of these figures) became canonical as "doctors" in the West: Saints Ambrose, Augustine, Gregory the Great, and Jerome. In the late thirteenth century, Pope Boniface VIII established a liturgical feast in honor of these four, thus adding to their fame for learning by giving them a place in the official liturgical calendar. In the 1568 edition of the Roman breviary, Pope Pius V added four names from the Eastern church (Saints Basil, Athanasius, Gregory Nazianzen, and John Chrysostom) to the feast of the Doctors of the Church. Those additions were symbolic in the sense that they were to highlight the unity of the early church by including names from both the East and the West.

None of the doctors named above lived later than the sixth century. When the scholastic theologians or monastic commentators of the Middle Ages spoke of the *doctores* they invariably meant those ancient patristic writers whose names were a guarantee of orthodoxy. Their opinions and interpretations carried a certain aura of ancient authority. Possibly as an apologetic move against the Reformers, the popes began to add to the list of doctors. In 1567 Pope Pius V, himself a Dominican, named his fellow Dominican, Saint Thomas Aquinas, as a Doctor of the Church. In 1588, the Franciscan Pope Sixtus V – perhaps in a desire for balance since the Dominicans and Franciscans have often been in competition with each other – named the Franciscan, Saint Bonaventure (an exact contemporary of Thomas Aquinas; they both died in 1274) to the canon of doctors.

In the same year, 1588, the Congregation of Rites (which had jurisdiction over canonizations and ancillary matters) articulated the criteria by which a person would qualify as a Doctor of the Church. In the eighteenth century, Prospero Lambertini (later Pope Benedict XIV) summarized those criteria in his now classic work on beatification and canonization which we discussed in chapter 3: a potential doctor should be a person of conspicuous holiness, a teacher of eminent doctrine, and be so named either by papal decree or a recognized General Council of the Church.

Thirteen more names were added to the list in the eighteenth century by various means: a direct apostolic letter from the pope; a simple decree by the Congregation of Rites assigning them a liturgical office; or, in the case of the Jesuit Peter Canisius (canonized in 1925), in the very documents of canonization. When Pope Pius XI named the Dominican Albert the Great (1206–1280) a Doctor of the Church he, in effect, also canonized him since Albert had been beatified in 1622 by Pope Gregory XV but had never been formally canonized. Both the cases of Peter Canisius and Albert the Great point to the close connection between canonization and the additional honorific of the title of Doctor.

Up until 1959 when the last one was so named (the little-known Capuchin Lawrence of Brindisi who died in 1619), all of the doctors were canonized saints (both some figures from the

Greek Church and one Syrian saint, Ephrem, named in 1920 are included) and all were men. That all changed in 1970 when Pope Paul VI named Saints Catherine of Siena (?1347–1380) and Teresa of Avila as Doctors of the Church; in 1997 Pope John Paul II added Saint Thérèse of Lisieux (1873–1897). Currently, the Roman Catholic Church honors thirty-three people as Doctors of the Church.[4]

One reason for the inflation of the number of doctors in the Roman Catholic Church was to demonstrate both continuing holiness in the church as well as the church's witness to theological and spiritual truth. In the post-Reformation church there was also the added desire to show that the world of saintly learning and teaching supported the claims of church unity under the papacy. This was nowhere more evident than in Gian Lorenzo Bernini's design for the Altar of the Chair of Peter in the Basilica of Saint Peter in the Vatican dedicated in 1665. This masterpiece of the Baroque consists of a huge throne (containing within it what is purported to be the apostle Peter's original *cathedra* or chair) held up by four figures. The two with episcopal miters represent Saints Ambrose and Augustine; those who are bare-headed are Saints Athanasius and John Chrysostom. Symbolically, the doctors of both the Western and Eastern churches hold up the authority of the papacy represented by the apostolic chair of Peter himself from whom all subsequent popes claim their lineage. To reinforce the point, the chair ensemble has above the throne a window depicting the Holy Spirit as a dove framed by billowing rays and cherubs in gilt stucco. In the late afternoon, the rays of the sun strike the window, sending beams of light down the long nave of the basilica. The entire work (or, as it was called in the Baroque period, a *concetto*) was a not too subtle statement fixing in bronze a glorification of the papacy sustained by the constant witness of the great doctors of antiquity.

There has been some discussion in the scholarly literature[5] about possible other inclusions into the category of Doctors of the Church. The present list includes figures whose doctrine is

Plate 6 The Altar of the Chair in St Peter's Basilica, Rome. Photo © 1990
SCALA, Florence.

now either of purely historical interest (for example, the moral
theology of the eighteenth-century theologian and bishop,
Alphonsus of Liguori) or not quite in the first rank of theology
(Saints Antony of Padua, Lawrence of Brindisi) so people have
discussed whether or not other appropriate names might merit
inclusion. If outstanding doctrine (i.e. teaching; the term means
more than dogmatic theology) includes spiritual teaching (as
it manifestly does in the case of Saint Thérèse of Lisieux, Saint

Teresa of Avila, and Saint Catherine of Siena) why not, for example, Saint Ignatius of Loyola? The further question, of course, is whether canonization is a sine qua non of the title. More adventuresome writers have even suggested some who are not Roman Catholic, like John Wesley. A more plausible candidate might be John Henry Newman (1801–1890), the nineteenth-century convert from Anglicanism who was the most supple Catholic theological mind of the nineteenth century. Since Newman's cause for canonization is in Rome perhaps he might be one who could be raised to the altars and declared a doctor at the same time.

The Starets

Byzantine spirituality has its deepest roots in the monastic tradition, respect for patristic teaching, and the liturgical life of the church. It has been a commonplace from the times of the earliest desert dwellers that anyone who wished to enter the monastic life should be formed by obedient instruction at the hands of an elder who has experience in the life. Monastic literature is full of cautionary tales about those who do not obey the elder and exemplary stories of those who listen to their instruction. To be a monk was to put oneself under the guidance of an *Abba*, a spiritual father or, in the case of women, a spiritual mother (*Amma*). In the tradition of Celtic monasticism, it was the "soul friend" (*Anamchara*) who performed a similar function. It was also a commonplace for people to come to those formed in and living out the monastic life to seek the counsel of those who had deep spiritual experience. The seeking of advice was so common that the questions asked of the elder had almost a stereotypical character to them. Some would ask for a "good word" or others would simply say: "What must I do?" Novice directors in religious orders today, both in the East and the West, are the latest incarnation of the ancient tradition of the spiritual father or mother, although this ancient tradition is still a hallmark of Orthodox monasticism.

The whole notion of the elder is rooted in a tradition that goes back to concepts in the New Testament as they were refined in later reflection; namely, that growth in Christian perfection paralleled human growth from infancy through young personhood to maturity. The warrant for such an idea comes from Paul's metaphor of growing to maturity and not being childish in the Christian life (see Eph. 4: 13–14) and of being fed on milk before being capable of meat (1 Cor. 3: 1–2). To that image the spiritual writers would also use the metaphors of climbing a ladder or taking a journey or ascending a mountain or passing through the desert to seek the Promised Land. Behind all of these images and metaphors is the idea of spiritual growth and progress under a sure guide.

This notion of being guided in the spiritual life is found in almost every strand of historical Christianity.[6] The person of the spiritual elder (Latin: *senex*; Greek: *geron*; Russian: *starets*) did not derive authority from ordination or monastic profession but from the charismatic power of holiness and experience. The elder could be a man or a woman. That indefatigable medieval traveler Margery Kempe tells us in her autobiography that she went to seek the counsel of the recluse Julian of Norwich about whom we know nothing save for her work *Showings*, one of the more important texts of medieval spirituality. The earlier *Ancrene Wisse* (a medieval rule of life for anchoresses) warns recluses not to give spiritual counsel to men – an admonition that would seem to imply that it was at least tolerable to provide such counsel to women. In the Roman Catholic Church, after Trent, spiritual direction was often seen as one task more for the confessional, even though the discrete practice of spiritual direction was also available for an elite minority.

From the late eighteenth century and down to our own day a refinement of the work of the elder developed in the Russian Church: the emergence of the *starets* (plural: *startsy*) in the monasteries of Russia. This new phenomenon, of course, has been immortalized by Fyodor Dostoevsky in *The Brothers Karamazov* in the person of Father Zossima who was thought to be modeled on an actual *starets* at the Optino Monastery, Father Ambrose, who served as a spiritual father from 1860 until his death in 1891.

Typically, a *starets* would begin life as a simple monk who followed the ordinary life of the monastery. After a period, such a monk would go into seclusion to follow a life of greater silence, prayer, fasting, and other ascetical practices. This period of self-imposed reclusion varied until the monk felt inspired to end his time of silence and, as the expression has it, "opened his doors" to receive visitors for counsel or other needs. Such a person would receive anyone who would come and listen to whatever need they brought to him: for spiritual advice, prayers for a particular need, healing from mental or physical affliction, or advice about his or her future direction. Such an elder attained that status not by some process of ordination but by the recognition of those who saw such a person as worthy enough to be approached. It was a charismatic office not an institutional one.

The nineteenth century was considered the Golden Age of the *startsy* in Russia. One of their number, Seraphim of Sarov (1759–1833), was canonized by the Russian Orthodox Church in 1903. His life was rather typical of the trajectory of a simple monk who developed into a great spiritual master. Prochoros Moshnin, born into a pious merchant family, entered the monastery of Sarov at the age of eighteen, taking the name of Seraphim. In 1786, at the age of twenty-seven, he took monastic vows and was ordained a deacon. Seven years later he was ordained a priest and thus became what was called a *hieromonk* – that is, a monk-priest. Already admired for his monastic fidelity and his austere style of life, he decided to retire to a forest hermitage about five miles from the monastery.

From 1796 until 1804 he lived in solitude, eating only vegetables and some necessities brought from the main monastery.

Plate 7 An icon of Saint Seraphim of Sarov (1759–1833). Fresco by Fr Simon Doolan of St Gregory of Sinai Monastery, California.

Twice he refused requests that he become an abbot of a monastery in need of a new abbot. In 1804 he came back to the monastery after having been beaten into a crippled state by robbers who chanced upon his forest hermitage. He recuperated for five months and returned to his hermitage, refusing an attempt to make him abbot of his own monastery in 1806. Four years later he went back to Sarov but maintained strict silence and seclusion until 1815. Inspired by a vision of the Blessed

Virgin, he "opened his doors" in that year and began to see visitors. The "opened doors" were a sign that he was available to anyone who would come to him for healing, prayers, spiritual counsel, and so on. He felt, as a result of another vision, that he should go again to his hermitage, but the monks built him a hut close to the monastery where he lived until he died. Contemporaries speak of daily crowds that came to visit him, which on certain feast days would swell into numbers as high as five thousand. He spoke to each visitor as "My Mother" or "My Father" or, his favored greeting, "My Joy."

Seraphim was widely regarded as a saint in his lifetime, and after his death in 1833 he was the object of a popular cult. People flocked to his grave site and icons were multiplied to honor his image. In 1903, Seraphim was solemnly canonized in the presence of thousands of the faithful who watched as the last tsar, Nicholas II, and the Grand Dukes of Russia carried his coffin to its fitting resting place. After the Revolution of 1917 the monastery was suppressed, but Seraphim of Sarov is still considered one of the most influential and popular saints of the Russian Orthodox Church. The writings that have come down to us (mainly recorded conversations with one of his disciples) have been judged by no less a person than the late Sergius Bolshakoff as the "summit of Russian mysticism."[7]

The tradition of the elder continues in our day. Father Amphilochios functioned as an elder on the isle of Patmos until his death in 1970. The Romanian elder Cleopas survived the persecution of his church in Romania, functioning as an elder until his death in 1998. The names of other such elders currently circulate in the Orthodox world, perhaps most famously Father Matthew the Poor who is a monk in Egypt. Matthew, whose writings are now beginning to be available in English,[8] entered the monastery of Saint Macarius in Egypt in 1948, carrying with him only a Bible, some writings of Isaac the Syrian, some empty notebooks for his own use, and an English translation of some sayings of the Russian and Greek Fathers. He devoted himself to a life of solitary contemplation and prayer; the fruits of that life now aid others, either through his writings or his spiritual counsel. Whether such persons will be canonized in the future is not clear today.

The Tractarians and the Saints

The Church of England, from its beginnings, carried within its tradition a tension between the evangelical impulses energized by the Reformation of the sixteenth century and its deep roots in the ancient Catholic faith so long a presence in the British Isles. In its history, one side of the tension would become more prominent than the other. In the first half of the nineteenth century, a group of mainly clerics associated with Oxford University attempted to call the Church of England back to its Catholic (but not necessarily Roman Catholic) roots. They were known as the Tractarians (or, more generally, the Oxford Movement) because their main means of dispersing their ideas was through a series of tracts on a wide range of topics concerned with church practice, polity, and theology. The tracts, which numbered ninety in all, ranged in length from a few pages to substantial monographs. The history of the complex firestorm that this movement unleashed is beyond the scope of this work, but the results of the movement may be succinctly stated. Some of the actors and their sympathizers left the Church of England and became Roman Catholics (most notably John Henry Newman in 1845), while others (for example, Edward Pusey) remained in the Anglican Communion. In the long run, the Tractarians did manage to influence large segments of the Church of England into a more Catholic direction (Anglican religious orders, for example, would be unthinkable except as seen against their movement) in liturgy, theology, and forms of spirituality, but the tensions between Low (i.e. evangelical) and High (i.e. Catholic) tendencies remain to this day within the Anglican Church. Perhaps the most lasting influence of the Tractarians and their successors was again to make the celebration of the Eucharist the center of Anglican worship, rather than the non-sacramental practice of Morning Prayer on Sunday.[9]

Of particular interest for our subject is a prospectus written by John Henry Newman in 1843, two years before he left the Church of England for the Roman Catholic Church, for a series of books to appear under the general rubric of *The Lives of the English Saints*. Newman saw this project as a natural follow-up of the infamous Tract no. 90 which he wrote arguing that the Thirty-nine Articles of the Anglican Church were not incompatible with Roman Catholic theology and practice even though some of the Articles may have had an anti-Roman bias.

Newman's fundamental intention in editing a series devoted to the English saints was to remind the people of his day that, before the sixteenth-century English split from Rome, there was an older tradition of Christian life and practice that was similar to that espoused by the Tractarians themselves. Newman thought that such a series of biographies would help his countrymen to remember that there was a national tradition of great saints whose memory had been largely lost after the Reformation. The lives of these saints, in short, would remind England that as a nation it had profoundly Catholic roots. As preparation for the series, Newman even drew up a calendar of saints, indicating their feast days for each month of the year. That list, done in 1843–4, was reprinted by Newman as a "note" to his edition of the *Apologia Pro Vita Sua* (1864). A quick glance at the list shows Newman drawing on names from the Anglo-Saxon period to the fifteenth century. He also developed a chronological list of saints from the second century (beginning with the legendary King Lucius) down to the fifteenth century.

In one sense it was a serendipitous time for such a series. The nineteenth century was a period in which there was something of a medieval revival, aided by the emergence of the Romantic movement. The novels of Walter Scott were best-sellers. Augustus

Pugin (died 1852) was at the forefront of the Gothic revival in English architecture. The Romantic writers showed a sympathy for the medieval. There had been two generations of interest in the Gothic as it was expressed in popular fiction. On the other hand, some of the contributors to Newman's series were more enthusiastic than judicious. Uncritically accepting the more flamboyant claims made in pious continental biographies drawn from the *legenda* of the saints, they accepted with little reflection stories of medieval miracles and other such extravagant phenomena. They showed an equal enthusiasm for ascetic practices, celibacy, and monasticism since they began the series with the strongly monastic saints of both the Anglo-Saxon period and the early Cistercians of the twelfth century. Many of the writers who would contribute to the series were themselves on the cusp of conversion to Rome and this added a polemical note to their approach to these lives.

The reaction of the educated reading public was predictable enough. They saw the books as a popish plot to undermine the national church. The exaltation of monastic vows and clerical celibacy flew in the face of the Victorian value of family life. More pertinently, the narratives of purported saintly miracles were greeted with skeptical derision. The issue of ecclesiastical miracles as recounted in the lives of the saints became the center of fierce polemics on both sides of the question. Newman became identified with the publications of the library of saints' lives (even though he quickly resigned the editorship) and, more pertinently, was forced to defend the possibility of such miracles.

When Newman did become a Roman Catholic in 1845 it was easy enough for his critics to point to *The Lives of the English Saints* as proof that he had already been a crypto-Catholic, selling to a credulous public and an impressionable undergraduate body all of the things that the national church had rebelled against in the first place: celibacy, monasticism, miraculous interventions through the power of the saints, and so on. Nearly two decades later, Newman still had to contend with the issue of medieval saints and their alleged powers of the miraculous in the exchange with Charles Kingsley that produced Newman's *Apologia Pro Vita Sua*. In that work, Newman set down the criterion by which such reports of miracles should be judged: "I say that they were to be regarded according to their greater or lesser probability, which was in some cases sufficient to create certitude about them, in other cases only belief or opinion." Newman held to that position to the end of his life.

It is interesting that in the final edition and revised version of the *Apologia* Newman felt constrained to add two appendices in which (in Note B) he discussed ecclesiastical miracles and, as we have seen, in Note D he reprinted the calendar of English saints upon which he hoped to base his proposed short biographies, as well as the prospectus he composed in 1843 to advertise the series. As if to make the point about the tradition of English saints more strongly, he reproduced the list again in chronological order, beginning with two saints who had connections with the British going back to the second century. As always, for Newman, the test was antiquity.[10]

His many critics, however, also held firmly to Article 22 of the Thirty-nine Articles which we had occasion to mention in chapter 3: "worshiping and adoration as well of images as of relics and also invocation of the saints is a fond thing, vainly invented, and grounded upon no warranty of Scripture, but rather repugnant to the Word of God." It is at least partially against this stricture that the reaction of much of the educated public must be understood.

When Newman became a Roman Catholic he, like all Catholics, venerated the saints. If there was one saint in particular to which Newman was firmly attached it was Saint Philip Neri who had founded the Oratory in Rome after which Newman modeled his own community of priests in Birmingham. Newman paid Philip Neri high praise in his ninth discourse on the idea of a university. He saw in Philip a model for his own priesthood. He praised him for his humility and unpretending love. In that wonderful prose which is Newman's mark, he says of Philip that, when he came to Rome from Florence, he:

> did not so much as seek his own as drew them to him. He sat in his small room, and they in their gay worldly dresses, the rich and wellborn, as well as the simple and illiterate, crowded into it. In the mid-heats of Summer, in the frosts of winter, still was he in that low and narrow cell at San Girolamo, reading the hearts of those who came to him and curing their souls' maladies by the very touch of his hand.

The project of *The Lives of the English Saints*, like many things Newman attempted in his Catholic days, was not a success. Nor were matters helped by the enthusiasm of some of the collaborators who translated or depended upon extravagant hagiographies imported from the continent. However, the celebration of saints' days did continue and continues in the Church of England. The sanctoral cycle tended to favor the saints of antiquity, but, slowly, saints from the English tradition (for example, Anselm of Canterbury) began to enter the Anglican calendar. Since the Anglican Church has no standing instrumentality for formal canonizations, that process has been done on a somewhat ad hoc basis with certain national churches within the Anglican Communion expanding the calendar of saints and others not doing so. Other forms of devotion or the use of saintly patrons for church organizations are common enough in the Anglican Communion today, largely as a long-term result of the Tractarian movement and its later analogues. Finally, the rise of Anglican monastic and religious communities for both men and women – almost all with roots in nineteenth-century Anglo-Catholicism – may be seen as a desire to "perform" the Christian life, either using a saint's life as a model (for example, among the various Anglican Franciscan communities) or by taking inspiration from the spiritual doctrine of a saintly founder (for example, following the Rule of Benedict).

The Tractarian turn to the Catholic roots of the Anglican Communion developed in the nineteenth century and has had deep resonances down to the present day. The "Catholic turn" (with antecedents in the seventeenth-century Caroline divines) anticipates similar turns, especially in the Lutheran tradition which never lost its liturgical roots in the older Catholic tradition. What developed from those turns will engage our attention in chapter 5.

Chapter 5

The Twentieth Century

They never forgot
That even the dreadful martyrdom must run its course . . .

W. H. Auden

Schools of Spirituality

One way in which the witness and work of some of the saints have persisted over the centuries is that their person, their performance of the path of Christian perfection in life, and their teaching have inspired others to follow their examples. If their memory has lingered long enough within the Christian tradition and there is a discernible spiritual ancestry to which we can appeal, they can be said to have founded a "school of spirituality." Even in our contemporary world there are people who commit themselves to a certain way of life either by joining a religious community or by aligning themselves with the spirit and spirituality of such a school. It is in this sense that we can speak of the Benedictine, Augustinian, Franciscan, Dominican, Carmelite, Salesian, or Ignatian schools of spirituality. Often these schools look back to a single founder or to a cluster of persons who lived at a certain time in a specific milieu (for example, the seventeenth-century French School).

In fact, in this more ecumenical age, Protestants often align themselves with the spirituality of monastic communities or various other religious communities to nourish their own Christian faith. Catholics, by turn, adopt practices from other traditions as witnessed by the enormous popularity of the prayer styles developed by the Protestant Taizé monastic community in France.

Mutatis mutandis, one can also speak of the Wesleyan, Lutheran, or Calvinist schools of spirituality. Perhaps it can be said with justice that schools of spirituality are the best evidence of the exemplary power of the great saints since many of the schools of spirituality derive their shape and theology from the performance of saintly founders.

A school of spirituality is something that must be understood as a good deal broader than a particular movement or a recent experiment in some kind of Christian exercise of piety. "Centering Prayer" is not a school of spirituality (even though it derives from one) nor is Taizé Prayer or the Alpha Course. Only persistence over time – a spiritual pedagogical tradition, if you will – allows us to speak meaningfully of a school of spirituality. It is in this historical sense that we will understand the term.

What constitutes such a school? It usually begins when a person or a small group of people (usually a master/mistress and some followers) gather together in order to live out the gospel in some particular fashion. Typically, such a person sees a need in the actually existent culture (for example, neglect of the poor, corrupt social or ecclesiastical structures, the need for education, a woeful lack of preaching, the felt need to enter into the life of prayer more deeply, or a desire to flee a corrupt culture) and begins an experiment in living. Quite frequently, that felt need derives from either an explicit or implicit desire for reform. From that person's example, his or her labors, or "way of life" arises a new way of life, some foundational documents, a cluster of writings, and the "reception" of this experiment in living by others. These beginnings of a tradition are then offered to the Christian community that receives it and it then enters into the living tradition of the church. As such a tradition persists over time, it take on the shape of a "school" that provides subsequent generations with a model for Christian living. Such a "school" has some salient features that distinguish one school from another one.[1]

It should be clear that such "schools" often derive from the intuitions of a saintly founder: hence the names of saints embedded in such adjectives as Franciscan, Dominican, Salesian (from Saint Francis de Sales), Benedictine, and so on. The "schools" derive their energy from the lives, teachings, and activities of the founders. In that sense, saintly founders are the starting-point of a putative school.

What are the characteristics of such a school? First, each school of spirituality has certain constants or emphases that give that school its defining shape. These constants come from what has been called a "source experience." Thus, for example, the monastic school deriving from the spirituality of Saint Benedict emphasizes the common life of the sharing of goods for advancing the life of prayer and work, while the Franciscan school stresses itinerancy, identification with the poor, and a love of personal, freely embraced, poverty. Such schools are typically manifested in the Roman Catholic Church in the persistence of a religious order. Historically, some of those orders have provided for a "third order," which is to say, lay persons who affiliate themselves with the order as a preferred way of living their life of Christian piety and practice. Others who are attracted to the "source experience" and its ramifications are not so formally attached to a given order but draw from the spiritual teachings of that order through informal associations such as retreats. However people affiliate themselves with a particular school, they extend in time the original insights of a Benedict, a Francis, or a Teresa of Avila. Hence the insights of a given saint are enfleshed for future generations. Such persons are "classics" in the sense that they possess an "excess of meaning."[2]

Second, each school of spirituality develops a certain way of praying and a particular focus on mission. Saint Ignatius of Loyola did not want his Jesuit followers to pray the liturgical office in common. He put an emphasis on meditative prayer in order to equip his followers to become "contemplatives in action." A person, whether Jesuit or not, learns the pedagogy of prayer first developed by Ignatius as expressed in his *Spiritual Exercises* which is now tailored for specific needs as cultural conditions change.[3]

Third, schools of spirituality develop either explicitly or implicitly pedagogical strategies to cultivate the life of prayer favored by a particular school. Carmelite prayer, for instance, has used the pedagogy developed by Saints John of the Cross and Teresa of Avila to foster contemplative prayer in a fashion quite different from Ignatian prayer or the liturgical life and meditative reading of Scripture emphasized in the Rule of Benedict. While a person might be a "freelance" practitioner of these forms of spirituality, the tradition itself strongly recommends the labors of a person already formed in a given tradition. Often, this pedagogy is supplied by having lay people somehow affiliated with the religious order in question. These "third-order" members have a long history behind them (Francis of Assisi developed a rule for them in his own lifetime), while others have arisen in modern times. Secular oblates are a feature of many Benedictine monasteries and the Cistercians (Trappists) have recently developed groups of "lay associates." Such persons live "in the world" but try to enrich their lives by the spiritual practices of the monastic house with which they affiliate. Many of these orders will designate a special person who aids the lay affiliates. Developing under such a guide is one of the primary tasks of spiritual direction. It is worthwhile noting in this regard that Saint John of the Cross, an acknowledged classical teacher of prayer, does not speak of spiritual directors but uses two other terms – teacher (Spanish: *maestro*) or guide (*guia*) – thus emphasizing the pedagogical nature of entrance into a serious spiritual way of life.

Fourth, each school of spirituality develops a "canon within the canon" – that is, certain texts from sacred Scripture become watchwords for a given school. Such schools do not restrict the canon, but they do privilege certain texts or clusters of texts as their rule of life. Schools that put a great emphasis on missionary outreach see themselves as "performing" the great mandate of Matthew's Gospel (Matt. 28: 18–20), while historically the contemplative orders have turned frequently to the commentary tradition of the Song of Songs in a trajectory that goes back to Origen of Alexandria. This "canon within the canon" privileges rather than excludes certain texts. One could argue that various schools of spirituality, shaped by their saintly founders, zero in on a cluster of texts against which they read the rest of Scripture. Distinct schools of spirituality are exercises in the living exegesis of certain scriptural texts, which they see as fundamental to their charism.

Fifth, schools of spirituality seek to cultivate intense spiritual experience and not simply notional ideas about the Christian life. The saint-founders maximally model such experiences, which provide the root for the shaping vision of a given school. While eternal salvation is probably the explicit ultimate goal of every Christian, it is possible to discern what experiences various schools hold up as a model of the vehicle for attaining that goal: identifying with the poor Christ (Saint Francis); doing the ordinary in an extraordinary way (Thérèse of Lisieux); learning to do all for the greater glory of God (Ignatius of Loyola); handing on the fruits of contemplative study (Saint Dominic and his followers); cultivating the love of God in one's state of life (Francis de Sales), and so on.

The many schools of spirituality within the larger Christian tradition point to the conservative nature of sanctity in the sense that the saint-founders demonstrate, in the words of the late Karl Rahner, that in *this particular way* it is possible to be a Christian and, once that way has been lived out, others may take it as a model for their lives.[4] The development of such schools, of course, are not only museum relics but ways of living today. Only the test of time will judge whether current movements in Christianity, inspired by the lives of our contemporaries and near contemporaries, will evolve into schools for the edification of future generations. These schools then draw upon the original insights developed by the saintly founders. The schools reflect difference within the larger Christian tradition. Their discrete experiences are offered to the larger church as one more way of living out the Christian experience.

In tandem with the rise and persistence of schools of spirituality are movements that take their inspiration from the example of saints and turn that example into some kind of practical plan of action. Frederic Ozanam (1813–1853), beatified in 1997, was a popular professor at the Sorbonne in Paris. Stung by a student's jibe that Christians were great at talk but slow with action, he gathered a small group of like-minded Catholics to deliver direct aid to the poor and to fight for human decency for the poor of Paris. Inspired by Saint Vincent de Paul, who had been the great seventeenth-century apostle to the poor of Paris, the small groups started by Frederic Ozanam outlived him. In many parts of the world, most parishes have Vincent de Paul societies consisting of small groups of parishioners who meet on a regular basis for prayer and to serve the poor directly with aid. In towns large enough, the same groups support larger outlets to help the needy by, for example, recycling clothes and furniture for those who cannot afford to shop in stores.

A New Saintliness?

Simone Weil (1909–1943) was one of those solitary seekers for the Absolute who could never find a natural home either in her native Jewishness or in the Christianity that had touched her so deeply. She remained an outsider looking for what she was convinced was a new kind of sanctity appropriate for the times in which she lived.[5] Deeply mystical, brilliant, and educated in the rarefied world of the French intellectual tradition (she was a schoolmate of both Simone de Beauvoir and Jean Paul Sartre), Weil identified herself with the poor, the estranged, and the persecuted. Temperamentally, she stands in a tradition that goes back to Søren Kierkegaard and her own countryman, Blaise Pascal. Weil is an influential figure for intellectuals even today, but more than anything else she was a single-minded spiritual pilgrim who, sensing the Otherness of God, stood, in her formulation, waiting in patience for God. She never would accept baptism, preferring to stand with all of the other outsiders on the margins of organized Christian life.

One can detect in Western culture in the twentieth century – a culture that has been famously described as seared by the acids of modernity – a longing for saintliness, albeit detectable in unexpected places. What kind of saintliness that might be can be framed by an exchange that Albert Camus gives us in his novel *The Plague*. A friend of the novel's hero, Doctor Rieux, says that he would like to be a saint. Rieux expresses his perplexity since his friend does not believe in God. "Ah," his friend responds, "that is the issue: how does one become a saint without believing in God?"

The issue of saintliness occurs frequently in the fiction of early and mid twentieth-century Europe. In Ignazio Silone's strongly anti-fascist novel *Bread and Wine*, the hero, Pietro Spina, confesses that he would love to be a saint if only he could be sure that old women would not pray before his statue and light candles in his honor. He assumes, as a disguise, the role of a priest, and the author leaves no doubt that he does consider his hero a saint but one who completely reverses the traditional role of the Catholic priest.

Graham Greene's *The Power and the Glory* takes up a similar theme. Greene frames his novel between two episodes in which a pious Mexican grandmother reads to her grandson about the life of a saintly martyr (loosely based on the life of Miguel Pro, SJ, who had died a martyr in 1920 in Mexico and was later canonized). She reads from a book exuding the typical clichés of such pious hagiographies. Greene's hero, an unnamed priest, is the very anti-type of such a conventional saint: he is a somewhat venal, alcoholic priest who has fathered an illegitimate son. His pursuer, the police lieutenant, is ascetic, celibate, uncorrupted politically, and a utopian reformer. In the end, the priest is shot, unshriven and trembling with fear (and longing for a drink to brace him up for his death) but clearly a true martyr. The under-lying motif of the book is the contrast between the priest's capa-city to love and the white-hot hatred of the police lieutenant.

Greene's novel is especially telling in that he frames its begin-ning and end by having an elderly grandmother reading a con-ventional hagiographical account of the life of a saintly martyr in Mexico based, roughly, on the life of the real-life martyr Miguel Pro, SJ, to stand in contrast to the "whisky priest" who is the real saint in Greene's estimation. Father Pro was executed before a firing squad in 1927. A famous photograph of him standing with his hands outstretched (Greene reproduces it in a travel book he wrote about Mexico) became a revered holy card in Mexico, especially since witnesses to his execution report that his last words were "Viva Cristo Rey!" (Hail, Christ the King!). Beatified in 1988, he stood for the unflinching heroism of an authentic martyr – in sharp contrast to the weak, but undoubt-edly saintly, alcoholic priest of Greene's imagination.

Each of the novels uses the imagery of the Bible (the literary critic Theodore Ziolkowski aptly calls them "Comrade Jesus" heroes)[6] and the language of sanctity to explore the theme of human transcendence for the greater good of humanity in a culture in which the traditional forms and language of religious faith do not seem capable of bearing up under the weight either of religious doubt or the might of powerful anti-religious pol-itical movements of both Left and Right. Their particular angle of vision reflects at least one element of the conception of saints in the twentieth century: namely, the saint as outsider both in terms of being outside traditional religious practice and also as witness *against* the politico-social situation which they consider inhumane and venomous.

The totally consumed, saintly figure of twentieth-century cul-ture has its antecedents in the writings of Friedrich Nietzsche who, in works like his aphoristic *Beyond Good and Evil*, held up the saintly figure as one whom others seek to emulate to understand fully their own human (and superhuman) potentiality. "The mightiest men have hitherto always bowed reverently before the saint, as the enigma of self subjugation and utter voluntary privation," he wrote in *Beyond Good and Evil*, because they saw in the saint "the superior force which wished to test itself by such a subjugation . . . they honored something in themselves when they honored the saint" (Aphorism no. 51).

In a peculiar but powerful work written in the 1930s, the Romanian intellectual E. M. Cioran, inspired by Nietzsche, read deeply in hagiography with special attention to those ecstatic saints who had the most powerful mystical experiences because they gave evidence of emotions that were, in the fashion he understood it, mystical, i.e. movements towards something beyond the empirical. That experience Cioran saw as the eruption of the Absolute into history. "Saintliness is a special kind of madness," Cioran wrote. "While the madness of mortals exhausts itself in useless and fantastic actions, holy madness is a conscious effort towards winning everything."[7] For Cioran, the great lesson of the saints is that they pressed beyond the usual desires of the human being by giving up their lives, or testifying with their bodies to unreachable goals, by pushing – here we borrow from Nietzsche – the limits of religious boundaries. Cannot one hear the life of Simone Weil in Cioran's judgment that belief in God as a sop to assuage loneliness is only a pretext, whereas the saint "knew how to be sad *for* God"?[8] In chapter 6 we will see how Cioran, in the 1930s, anticipates the idea of sainthood studied by contemporary postmodern thinkers.

This kind of thinking has a nineteenth-century pedigree in which the saint is conceived as a titanic figure who overcomes self in search of something beyond. It is clearly in Nietzsche; it is behind Gustave Flaubert's *The Tentation de Saint Antoine*; in the writings of the Decadents; it flourishes in Cioran and Weil; it shows up in the fiction of Nikos Kazantzakis; and marks one of the ways in which the issue of saintliness continues to fascinate the intellectual world.

Others in the twentieth century have sought for saintly persons outside the confines of formal canonization processes or other ecclesiastical seals of authenticity. Although deeply touched by the Tolstoyan Christianity of the Beatitudes which he encountered as a student in England, Mohandas Gandhi (1869–1948), the energizing force of Indian independence, was not a Christian, even though he has been honored by the sobriquet of saint by Christians and called by his own people "The Great Soul." If Gandhi married a certain strand of Christianity to his own profound grasp of Hindu themes of non-violence, it was this worldview, so effective in India, that inspired Martin Luther King, Jr, to shape his struggle for civil rights in the United States into a campaign of non-compliance to segregation laws and non-violence as a way of protest. King was a martyr to those views but, in turn, provided inspiration to others to use similar means in places as different as South Africa and Eastern Europe. Almost by analogy, one could say that Gandhi started a "school" of the spirituality of non-violence which still resonates today both inside and beyond India. Gandhi is an interesting case study if for no other reason than that his story is an interwoven tale in which Christianity and Hinduism meet in a new synthesis of selfless love.

Within the Christian tradition itself, Dr Albert Schweitzer (1875–1965) left a brilliant academic career as a theologian and an equal reputation as an authority on the music of Bach to study medicine and go to Africa as a missionary doctor. He would remain there in Gabon for the rest of his life working with the sick poor as his personal act of atonement for what he saw as the sins of colonialism. The 1958 winner of the Nobel Prize for peace as the exponent of his philosophy of "reverence for life," his personal witness for the gospel was a performative act that went far beyond his own trenchant critical scholarship on the New Testament or his justly famous work as a musicologist.

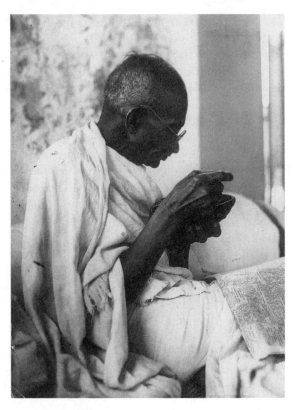

Plate 8 Mohandas Gandhi (1869–1948). Photo © Walter Bosshard / Hulton
Archive / Getty Images.

The saint as outsider does not sum up all that can be said
about saintly persons in the twentieth century, but it does represent a type to which the title of "saint" has been used by social
commentators. For one who represents the older paradigm of
the saint (although not yet canonized, she was beatified in 2003),
who has received worldwide recognition, one might consider
the Nobel laureate, Mother Teresa of Calcutta (1910–1997). In
a sense, Mother Teresa fits one of the most ancient profiles

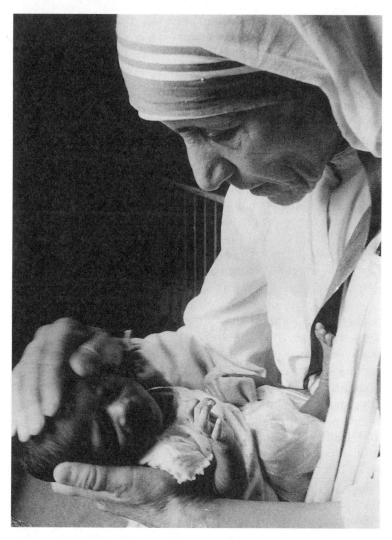

Plate 9 Mother Teresa of Calcutta (1910–1997). Photo © Hulton Archive /
Getty Images.

of the traditional Catholic saint. In 1946, after twenty years of conventional convent life in Calcutta as a teacher, Mother Teresa claimed that she "saw" in a very deep way the suffering poor of India for the first time. Receiving permission to leave her convent to serve them, she began a life-long commitment to those dying in the streets of the city. After some years of this labor she began to be recognized by the larger public for her work. She was the subject of television documentaries, newspaper accounts, books, and so on. As her own congregation (The Missionaries of Charity) grew, she expanded her work around the world, attracting both many aspirants to her community and a legion of supporters and sometime volunteers.

Mother Teresa taught and lived a very traditional Catholic spirituality and was equally traditional in her theology and practice. She would not countenance professional fund-raising in her name, carefully screened those who had contact with her sisters as confessors and teachers, demanded that her sisters live a poor life, and resolutely resisted any moral compromise on issues such as abortion and euthanasia (as she made clear in her 1979 Nobel speech). All things being equal, she fits the profile of many religious women who have been canonized over the past centuries: doctrinally orthodox, a personal life of heroic virtue, a boundless charity towards others, and the title of foundress. If anything, the life and work of Mother Teresa shows that the traditional life of the saintly person can prove attractive to many and, further, given the easy availability of the mass media, can exemplify that kind of sanctity on a world stage. There was a sad irony in the fact that this world-renowned figure died and was buried in the same week as the funeral events attendant upon the death of Princess Diana.

Similarly, the American Dorothy Day (1897–1980) represents a person who went through the acids of modernity. Prior to her conversion, she had a colorful life as a journalist, screenplay writer, and novelist who had her share of love affairs (and one abortion) before embracing Catholicism in 1926 after the birth of her daughter. A co-founder of the Catholic Worker Movement, she was a pacifist and social activist who managed to combine an intense traditional Catholic piety with her own brand of radicalism. Frequently jailed for her non-violent protests, she herself brushed aside well-meaning people who called her a "saint." "When they call you a saint," she once remarked, "it basically means that they do not have to take you too seriously." Many Catholic Workers today are not too pleased by the possibility of her canonization, thinking that the monies spent on the process would be better used for the alleviation of the sufferings of the poor.

It should be noted that Dorothy Day drew heavily on the tradition of the saints to flesh out her own way of life. She greatly loved Francis of Assisi for his love of the poor, Saint Benedict for his sense of the liturgical life, and Thérèse of Lisieux (whose biography she wrote) for her doctrine of finding God's will by doing the ordinary in an extraordinary fashion. Day, as a pacifist, also took inspiration from the Gandhian doctrine of non-violence.

The New Martyrs

It has been argued by more than one scholar that more Christians died because they were Christians in the twentieth century than all those who died over the course of the three centuries of Roman persecution.[9] The genocidal attacks on the Armenian Christians by the Turkish government, the wholesale disappearance of Christians into the Soviet gulags from the 1920s onwards, the persecution of Christians in the period of National Socialism in Germany, the ruthless suppression of Christians in China after the Communist takeover of that country, and the history of Christian suffering in many Islamic countries which goes on apace, would add up to deaths in the millions.

One other feature of anti-Christian violence in the contemporary world has been the homicidal attacks on Christians by other Christians with the persecutors carrying out their violence in the name of Christian values or Christian culture. History has shown us many examples of this kind of violence in Latin and Central America and, sporadically, in Europe and elsewhere.[10] Clearly, not all those who died as Christians (and, it is well to remember, that in this period "Christians" also must answer for violence against others!) died as martyrs in the technical sense of the term. Many persons went to their death because they were the victims of ethnic hatred or were potential enemies of political power struggles. In some instances, there was killing of Christian by other Christians based on deep political and social divisions as was (is) the case in Northern Ireland and in the former Yugoslavia where Orthodox and Catholic partisans struggle for political and economic hegemony.

In the Roman world the case for martyrdom was clear. Christians suffered and died because in the minds of the Romans they did not show *pietas* to the Roman pantheon of gods and, in that refusal, seemed to be a treacherous fifth column undermining the legitimacy of the Roman state. By embracing Christ alone, they undermined the legitimacy of Jupiter. In our times, the matter is more complex. The 1998 canonization of Edith Stein (her religious name was Teresa Benedicta of the Holy Cross) by Pope John Paul II as a martyr raised this question in a very acute way: did she die in the gas chambers of Auschwitz because she was a Carmelite nun or because she was a Jew? Similarly, some German Christians seemed unwilling to call the Lutheran pastor and theologian Dietrich Bonhoeffer (1906–1945) a "martyr" because he was executed for political reasons even though he had worked out a theological rationale for resisting the Nazi government even before the beginning of World War II. Finally, were those lay people, religious sisters, priests, and bishops (like Oscar Romero) who were assassinated by the death squads in El Salvador Christian martyrs or the targets of political assassins?

In the common currency of religious language, such people have been regarded as martyrs at least in the broad sense that

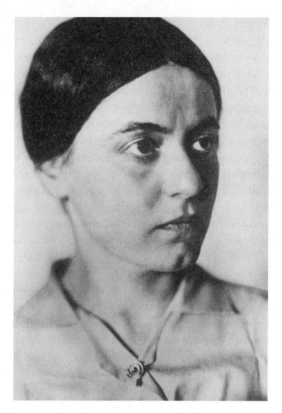

Plate 10 Edith Stein (Teresa Benedicta of the Holy Cross, 1891–1942). Photo AKG-Images.

their lives were witness to truth against falsity and love against hate. Theologians as early as Thomas Aquinas and as recently as Karl Rahner have asked for a more generous understanding of martyrdom as a complex response to death involving fortitude, faith, love, and a willingness to die for truth. Pope John Paul II has argued in a number of places that the best evidence of Christian ecumenism is to be found in the martyrs of the twentieth century – Catholic, Protestant, and Orthodox – who have given up their lives in defense of the gospel and for the fundamental truths that guarantee the dignity of all people. In his 1995 encyclical letter on Christian ecumenism (*Ut Unum Sint*), the pope wrote that "In a theocentric vision, we Christians already have a common martyrology. This also includes the martyrs of the present century, more common than one might think, and it shows, at a profound level, God preserves communion among the baptized in the supreme demand of faith, manifested in the sacrifice of life itself" (paragraph no. 84). To underscore how serious the pope was about that conviction, he asked that a martyrology of the twentieth century be compiled as part of the celebrations for the new millennium in 2000.[11] Such compilations have already been undertaken but no definitive list has appeared in print.

A fair example of the kind of twentieth-century martyr Pope John Paul II had in mind was symbolized by the mass beatification of twenty-seven people in the Ukraine who were killed between 1923 and 1963 either by the emergent power of Soviet Russia or during the Nazi invasion of the Ukraine during World War II. In the list were Latin and Eastern rite prelates, priests, women religious, and a lay person, who had suffered either under the Soviet government or at the hands of the Nazis. They stood symbolically as representatives of those who suffered as Christians in Eastern Europe in the twentieth century.[12]

Those who did die precisely as Christians protesting the inhumanity of tyrannical political systems function as prophetic figures who stood for the teachings of Jesus against either the passivity of those who acquiesced to regnant power (as in the case of Nazi Germany where the track record of Christians protesting the Nazis was modest) or as solitary figures who made up a small voice in a near totally hostile culture (the Christian minority in countries like Pakistan). The Central American liberation theologian, Jon Sobrino, has developed the neologism "Jesuanic" martyrs for such persons; that is, those who died like Jesus alone and at the hands of hostile powers. When we remember the active martyrs, we should not forget the many thousands of

Plate 11 Westminster Abbey's homage to the contemporary martyrs. Photo Topham Picturepoint.

passive martyrs (the Jesuanic martyrs about whom Sobrino has written) – the disenfranchised who simply "disappeared," dead who remain nameless.[13]

One concrete manifestation of the ecumenical range of contemporary active martyrs may be seen in the ten sculptured figures installed in niches over the western portal of Westminster Abbey blessed in 1998 by the then Archbishop of Canterbury, George Carey, at a ceremony attended by Queen Elizabeth II. Those figures, meant to be representative of the larger reality of modern Christian martyrdom, include persons from the Russian Orthodox, Roman Catholic, Anglican, Presbyterian, Lutheran, and Baptist Churches. The decision to fill these hitherto empty niches with modern martyrs instead of historic saints or allegorical figures was made precisely to point out that Christians have died and continued to die for the sake of the gospel. Furthermore, the figures were chosen to represent martyrs who have died in places as diverse as Papua New Guinea, Pakistan, Africa, and China, as well as those in Europe and North America. By stressing the modern world, the intention was to show the continuity of the Christian tradition, which began as a persecuted church but still sees persecution and the witness of martyrs to this day.[14]

When Karol Wojtyla was elected pope in 1978 he was the first person from Eastern Europe ever to be elected as the Bishop of Rome. As a native Pole he had personal experience of the realities of both National Socialism and Stalinist Communism. He trained for the priesthood in a clandestine seminary under Nazi occupation and his priestly ministry was exercised in the hostile environment of a Communist state. Those experiences had a shaping influence on his view of life when he assumed the papacy. Most scholars agree that he had a significant role in the demise of the Communist hegemony over the Iron Curtain countries in general and Poland in particular.

In 1983 John Paul II issued an apostolic constitution entitled *Divinus Perfectionis Magister* (The Divine Teacher of Perfection), radically modifying the procedures for beatification and canonization that had been in place since the days of Benedict XIV. The most significant shift in procedure was that the burden of investigation in the canonization process now rested with the bishop of a local church. It was his task (or, most commonly, that of a person deputed by him, called the *postulator*) to investigate the life and writings and witnesses (should they be alive) of a candidate known by the term "servant of God." A scrupulous investigation is carried out until such time as the bishop or postulator feels ready to compile a complete dossier along with letters assuring the Roman authorities that no illicit cult of the person has been in place. This dossier is forwarded to Rome along with copies of the person's writings. The dossier falls under the competence of the Sacred Congregation for the Causes of Saints (formerly part of the Congregation of Rites) which is the office deputed to handle the canonization process.

When the dossier comes to Rome it continues as part of the same process begun at the local level. A scholar who is part of the congregation, known as the *relator*, is appointed who, with the aid of others, develops, as it were, a complete biography of the person along with a report on the person's life of heroic virtue and doctrinal soundness (known as the *Positio*). When the complete *Positio* has been reviewed by competent theologians, it is presented to the officials of the congregation along with reports of purported miracles (requiring expert medical judgments). One miracle is needed for beatification, a second for canonization. The officials in time make their report to the pope who alone has the right to decree that a public cult may be established. The beatification or canonization ceremony itself is a proclamation by the pope that the person is inscribed in the catalog (canon) of the saints. In beatification, the cult of the saint is local; in canonization, the saint is proposed for the universal church.[15]

Pope John Paul's reform of the procedures for beatification and canonization was made with the express desire of rooting the procedure more closely to the life of the local church, even though the final stages of the process are accomplished in Rome, with the pope alone (as has been true since the twelfth century as we have seen) able to actually proclaim a beatification or canonization.

The reforms initiated by John Paul II were not only done for reasons of streamlining the otherwise cumbersome canonization process. The pope has revitalized the process of canonization in order to allow him to beatify and canonize saints at a much faster rate. In fact, John Paul II has beatified and/or canonized more people in his papacy than all the popes combined in the period since the Catholic Reformation of the sixteenth century. The list of his beatifications and canonizations are inching up to nearly nine hundred as of the year 2003. The prodigal use of this process has been the subject of some wonder and criticism, both in Rome and in other parts of the church. The criticism comes mainly from those (including some in the Roman curia) who think both that the process is too hasty and that the multiplication of new saints cheapens the whole notion of those who are in the canon of the saints.

What is the papal reasoning behind this expansion of canonizations? Judging from his own remarks in his speeches and in his writings, one can detect a number of reasons. First, the pope has an apologetic reason for canonizing saints. He wishes to show that there is a continuing witness to the possibility of the life of holiness in the church, not only historically but actually. He is especially keen on the witness of the martyrs because their sacrificial lives demonstrate that the truth of the gospel is precious enough to die for. The 1984 murder of Father Jerzy Popieluszko, the priest who was a hero to the Solidarity Movement in Poland, was a nodal point for the overthrow of the Communist government, which took place five years after his death. He constantly preached the message that good could overcome evil. His grave site today is like a shrine where he is honored as a martyr.

Next, the pope has had a consistent predilection for canonizing saints from regions other than the traditional geographical locations of Europe or the Middle East where saints have typically been found. He wants to show – by canonizing people from the Far East, India, Oceania, and so on – that the possibility of sanctity may be found in all places where the Catholic Church has been planted. Such canonizations, in his estimation, testify to the wide world of Christian holiness.

Thirdly, canonizations are pedagogical by their very nature. They often "send a message" which can be benign (this or that person represents martyrs in a particular country) or they can be quite pointed. Some of the recent papal canonizations have held up values for which the pope has a strong and abiding interest. It did not hurt the cause of Saint Maximilian Kolbe (1894–1941), a heroic figure in Auschwitz who volunteered to stand in for a married man who had been condemned to die in a starvation bunker, that he was a conservative, zealous, Polish priest who shared the papal penchant for a kind of baroque devotion to the Blessed Mother. The recent canonization of the founder of the reactionary movement known as Opus Dei was an eyebrow-raising moment for many people, but everyone knew of the papal approval of their stern view of Catholic life and practice. Many press reports also have noted the intense pressure that Opus Dei exercised in forwarding the canonization. It has also been said, somewhat waggishly, that the quickest way to get a papal visit to a particular country is to have someone whose canonization process is nearing completion since the pope loves to canonize in situ and not only in Saint Peter's Basilica where most canonizations traditionally take place.

Anglican and Lutheran Calendars

The traditional Protestant resistance to the cult of the saints, at least in some liturgically oriented denominations, eroded somewhat in the twentieth century under the influence of the Tractarians, in the case of the Anglican Communion, and from a more general desire to examine the older Catholic roots from which the Reformation grew. This shift has also been helped by the serious ecumenical dialogue that has been going on in the wake of Vatican II.[16] In non-Roman Catholic or Orthodox liturgical books one begins to see the appearance of commemorations for saintly figures.

In 1979 the Episcopal Church in North America adopted, not without controversy, an amended *Book of Common Prayer* which superseded the revision of the prayer book of 1928. The calendar of the church year outlined in the *Book of Common Prayer* distinguishes moveable feasts (computed in relation to Easter) and fixed feasts like Christmas Day. It further designates other majors feasts both of Our Lord and feasts commemorating the Blessed Virgin Mary, the angels, apostles, and national days like Thanksgiving and Independence Day. Finally, it allows for optional observances which do not conflict with Sundays and majors feasts. These optional observances are listed in the calendar of the church year. It is an interesting calendar to inspect since it lists outstanding figures in the Christian church some of whom are canonized saints of the Roman Catholic Church (for example, Francis of Assisi, Catherine of Siena) and the Orthodox Church (Saint Sergius, also in the Roman martyrology). Finally, it remembers outstanding and holy figures of the Anglican Communion who, while never formally canonized (there is no standard procedure for canonization), are conspicuous for their holiness and probity of life.

These figures seem to have been chosen to reflect the range of holiness in the Anglican tradition. Proto-Anglicans like William Tyndale, Hugh Latimer, Nicholas Ridley, and Thomas Cranmer are present as are great seventeenth-century divines like Richard Hooker, Lancelot Andrewes, Jeremy Taylor, and William Laud, as well as the poet-priests George Herbert and John Donne. The Anglican priests John and Charles Wesley are commemorated, as well as conspicuous figures associated with the Oxford Movement like Edward B. Pusey and John Keble. Nineteenth-century martyrs like the native Rhodesian catechist Bernard Mizecki, the martyrs of Eastern equatorial Africa, and those who died in Melanesia are listed, as well as those murdered during World War II by the Japanese in New Guinea.

The *Lutheran Book of Worship*, prepared by the Inter-Lutheran Commission on Worship in 1978, is the liturgical service book of the Lutheran Church of America, the American Lutheran Church, the Evangelical Lutheran Church of Canada, and the Missouri Synod Lutheran Church. This book allows for "commemorations" in the monthly calendar which may be "observed as desired." The general instructions go on to say that "local custom may suggest the addition of further commemorations." Under the rubric of "commemoration" are the following headings: saints, martyrs, pastors, bishops, missionaries, renewers of the church, theologians, renewers of society, artists and scientists. Commemorations are never given precedence over the annual church cycle or the major or minor feasts of the church.

A superficial glance at the church calendar reveals that it not only names a wide range of heroic Christians but designates under which category they are to be commemorated. Thus, Martin Luther King, Jr, is designated as a renewer of society and martyr, while John and Charles Wesley are called renewers of the church. A fair sprinkling of Roman Catholic saints like Thomas Aquinas and Gregory the Great merit commemorations, while in the month of April Albrecht Dürer and Michelangelo Buonarroti are honored as, respectively, painter and artist on April 6, and the theologian Dietrich Bonhoeffer is commemorated three days later as teacher but, oddly, not as martyr. On July 28 both Johann Sebastian Bach and George Frideric Handel are mentioned as musicians, while August sees the name of Florence Nightingale as a renewer of society, and a month later, in September, the late secretary general of the United Nations, Dag Hammarskjöld, as peacemaker.

Even from this cursory glance at the Lutheran calendar it is clear that the Lutheran perspective does not operate within the strict category of saints as the historic tradition understands the term. The approach of the Lutheran liturgical calendar is to highlight outstanding Christians of the past to indicate the manifold ways in which they lived out their faith. This understanding also allows for wide latitude in the choice of commemorations to fit the needs of local congregations. This flexibility becomes clear when one looks at the Spanish language Lutheran liturgical book developed by the Evangelical Lutheran Church of America (ELCA) in 1998, *Libro Liturgia y Cantico*. Not only does this work allow for regional rituals like the Mexican celebration of *Las Posadas* for Christmas (beginning on December 16) but it adds to the calendar such notable figures as the Salvadoran (Roman Catholic) bishop-martyr, Oscar Romero. Similarly, the ELCA and the Missouri Synod Lutheran Church produced, in 1999, a liturgical book for African American congregations under the title *This Far by Faith: An African American Resource for Worship*. This book contains a section under the title "Witnesses to the Faith" which provides roughly twenty-five brief biographies of notable African and African American Christians, ranging from the early desert fathers like Moses the Black through the late medieval saint Benedict the African (died 1589) to contemporary figures like Emma Francis, who was the first black Lutheran deaconess in the United States.

The preface to the section "Witnesses to the Faith" gives the clearest rationale for such commemorations in the Lutheran tradition. Drawing on the Apologia to the Augsburg Confession, the editors note how people of faith may honor exemplary Christians of previous generations: by giving thanks to God for their lives and witness; by allowing their example to motivate people today; and by entrusting one's own spiritual growth to the "abounding grace of God." Quite clearly, such an approach remains rightly consonant with the Reformation's resistance to any concept of the saint as intercessor.

The Methodist Church observes the calendar of the Christian year beginning in Advent and concluding with the Sundays after Pentecost but does not typically allow for the commemoration of individual saints. The North American *United Methodist Hymnal* (1989) does indicate a selection of hymns, psalms, and canticles appropriate for the celebration of All Saints Day but this reflects a celebration of the creedal affirmation of faith in the communion of saints. If other commemorative days are observed (for example, a festival for the feast of Saint Francis of Assisi), it is typically done on an ad hoc basis at the discretion of the local community.

Chapter 6

The Saints, World Religions, and the Future

Test saintliness by common sense . . .

William James

This brief volume has extended its narrative about Christian saints from the witness of the martyrs in the period of the Roman persecutions down to the present age. In this overview of the saintly horizon we have met heroic persons of charity, founders of schools of spirituality, emblematic figures of virtue, and personages whose history we can scarcely recognize because the accounts of their lives are obscured by a patina of folklore and fictional yearning. Beyond falling back on the rubric of inclusion in the canon of officially recognized saints in a given Christian tradition as a test of what constitutes a saint, we are no closer to a clear definition of the saint than we were at the beginning of this study. Perhaps the best we can do is to say that the category of saint is so generic that we can only call a person a saint because we recognize that this or that person belongs under that title, i.e. that this or that person bears a "family resemblance" (I am again using Wittgenstein's vocabulary) to what we consider a saint to be. Such an approach permits us to think of saints beyond the boundary of those who belong on some authorized roll (canon) recognized by an ecclesiastical body within Christianity. After all, the term "saint" is frequently used of persons in a religious tradition even when that person is not officially recognized as such.

Within Christianity itself it is hard to disentangle all of the strands that go to make up the portrait of the saint. We probably need to distinguish "emblematic" saints, about whom we know nothing reliable, but who "stand" for something symbolically, as in the case of Saint Christopher and safe travel or Saint Apollonia who is invoked against toothache, as opposed to those about whom we know a great deal who could serve as models of Christian life and practice. The saints have historically played a great role in the history of art, but it has only been in passing that we have touched on the great tradition of religious iconography (see Appendix II). The day has long passed when most people would recognize the symbols that distinguish one saint from another in a stained-glass window. Yet, in the past, ordinary folks would be able to distinguish Saint Barbara with her tower from Saint Catherine of Alexandria with her wheel. Many would have known the folktales connected to the saints which explain why Saint Lawrence is shown with a grill or Saint Christopher with a child on his shoulder or Saint Peter clutching his keys. Nor have we even touched on the sociology of sainthood beyond a passing reference to who gets canonized and why males outnumber females in the lists of medieval saints.

We have attempted an incomplete taxonomy of the "kinds" of saints that exist in the Christian tradition but have produced nothing like a complete phenomenology of sainthood itself. Readers who have persisted in reading to this point already know that the concept of the saint is theologically a controversial one, with whole segments of the Christian world rejecting the notion of saints (especially canonized ones) that are characteristic of both the Roman Catholic and Orthodox worlds. Finally, there is the specialized world of historical interpretation where, as the Bollandists have known for centuries, the dissection of history from legend and folklore is not always an easy one. This specialized world has given birth to an entire field of scholarly inquiry. Furthermore, a whole new field of research, energized by gender studies and political theory, has gone back to the legends of the saints for reasons other than spiritual or theological ones.

Which brings us to another question to which we can say a word: is the saint peculiar to the Christian tradition? We briefly brushed against this question in chapter 5 when we noticed that in the modern period the term "saint" began to be used in the world of fiction for people who were decidedly not orthodox Christian believers; indeed, some were not believers at all. Furthermore, we noted that the term was used of people, like Mohandas Gandhi who, while not unsympathetic to Christian claims, were not Christians in any usual sense of the term. In both of those instances, however, it is the largely Christian West that has applied the terminology of the "saint" to such figures whether fictional or real.

It is also the case, and recent scholarship has studied this fact assiduously, that other religious traditions mark out persons who function in certain analogous ways – whether as models or intercessors or exemplars or miracle workers – to those who are described as saints in the Christian tradition.[1] Given the clear fact of the presence, in large numbers, of believers of traditions like Islam, Hinduism, Jainism, Buddhism, and Sikhism in the contemporary West, it would be negligent if we did not pay attention to the tradition of the holy person (that generic term will serve for the moment) in those traditions. We should be sensitive to the simple fact that when we use the term "saint" to describe someone of another religious tradition, we should be careful not to do so in an imperialistic fashion so as to impose on another tradition language which is very much and peculiarly our own. What may count for a saint in the West may well have a quite different significance elsewhere in the world.

Some Terminology

While it is true that we must be careful not to superimpose the term "saint" on traditions that would not feel comfortable with the use of the term in any but a generic sense, it is also true that religious traditions do recognize conspicuous persons as models in life, conduits of sacred power, and as intercessors after death, to whose tombs the pious come in order to pray, seek favors for intercession, and piously remember their memory. Thus, in Judaism, for example, the Hasidic tradition recognizes certain holy rabbis who are known as the "Righteous Ones" (Hebrew: *tzaddikim*) or the sages whose reputation for spiritual power is such that their tombs are venerated and their intercession sought, even though there is nothing approaching a formal process of canonization. They may even possess some of these "saintly" qualities in their own lifetime. Rather like the spontaneity found in early Christianity, they are venerated in life for their holiness and, among Hasidic Jews, their tombs become holy places after their death where people will come to offer their intercessory prayers. To this day, pious Hasidic Jews flock to a New York cemetery on the anniversary of the death of Menachem Mandel Schneerson, the head of the Lubavicher Hasidic Movement to pray for the aid of their *rebbe* who died in 1994. Some of his followers even think that he will return as the promised Messiah of Israel even though that aspiration has somewhat split the unity of the group.

The "Righteous Ones" of Hasidic Judaism seem very much like Christian saints in the traditional sense of the term. They may stand out as a "type" but long before the Hasidic Movement there was a recognition of exemplary types who serve as models and exemplars of Israel's faith. There are the great patriarchs and matriarchs as well as the seers and prophets who were held up as models of fidelity to Torah values. The Book of Sirach (Ecclesiasticus) has a famous section beginning with the well-known trope "Let us now sing the praises of famous men /

our ancestors in their generations" (Sir. 44: 1) which then continues for six lengthy chapters lauding the great virtues and deeds of Old Testament figures from Enoch to "Josiah and other Worthies."[2]

Even though the two books of the Maccabees, like Sirach, were not included in the Palestinian canon (and hence are not regarded as canonical scriptures in Judaism even though the books are part of the Greek Septuagint), they are accepted as canonical in the Catholic tradition. Part of the importance of the two books of Maccabees for our discussion is that in Second Maccabees there are accounts of those who suffered martyrdom for the sake of Torah under the hands of pagans before the Christian era. The story of Eleazar (2 Macc. 6: 18–31), who died rather than violate the laws of Kosher, and the violent deaths of the Jewish mother and her seven sons (2 Macc. 7) became, in the estimation of some scholars, the literary models for the earliest Christian martyrologies. Those martyrs, as the narrator of Second Maccabees wrote of Eleazar, became a "model of courage and an unforgettable example of virtue not only for the young but for the whole nation" (2 Macc. 6: 31).

A somewhat similar practice to that of the "Righteous Ones" of Judaism may be found in the tradition of Sufism in Islam. The so-called "Friends of God" (Arabic: *awliya*), who are mentioned in the Qur'ān (*Sūra* 10: 63), are understood in a particular fashion in the Sufi tradition. Such figures are venerated in many Islamic countries and in some places are especially popular objects of cult. They are venerated as miracle workers and accepted as powerful mystics whose tombs, after their deaths, are the destination of the pious and considered as holy places by the faithful. The etiology of such practices may have been influenced by Christianity, although this has been the subject of much debate.

Both the "Righteous Ones" in Judaism and the "Friends of God" in Islam grew out of a veneration of those who are living paradigms of their respective faiths. In that sense they were

iconic figures of holiness (i.e. closeness to God). In time, super-
natural powers were associated with their persons both during
and after their earthly lives. In circles that venerate such figures,
it is clear that their power extends beyond the terrestrial realm
so that they serve as conduits of grace and power.

Both in Judaism and Islam the tradition of cults associated
with burial sites is very much a minority practice frowned on by
the majority of their co-religionists. Such practices are seen as
forms of deviant behavior by the majority who prefer to look at
the best exemplars of their faith traditions under the rubric of
living repositories of religious practice. It should be further noted
that while Buddhism in its pure doctrinal form sees the Buddha
as the one who points the way and not an end in himself,
nonetheless his person is venerated in Buddhist temples and
shrines, his relics are powerful sources of grace, and the places
associated with his name are the destinations of pilgrimage and
veneration. The Buddhist tradition of the *Bodhisattva*, an enlightened one who remains in this world to aid others, is quite often
a person venerated after death. The same could be said of certain personages in both the Hindu and Jain traditions.

What the majority of the world's historical religions do hold
in common is the acceptance of certain persons as profound
repositories of religious wisdom. Some saints in the Christian
tradition are held up for veneration not because of their miraculous powers or as intercessory figures but because of their
profound grasp of the Christian faith: a saint like Jerome or
Thomas Aquinas immediately comes to mind as an exemplar of
this understanding of the saint. These wisdom figures become
paradigmatic precisely because they possess a deep grasp of the
datum of faith as experienced in life. The category of "Doctors of
the Church," discussed in chapter 4, has as its precise aim to
highlight wisdom teaching.

The category of wisdom is found in many other traditions.
Thus, to cite some obvious examples: the sage in Judaism or the
sadhu in the Jain tradition who has become a "Great Soul" by

attaining enlightenment. Other traditions venerate similar figures: the enlightened *Arahant* in Theravada Buddhism or the perfected one in Hinduism known as the *Siddha* or the one who has attained enlightenment but remains in the world to guide others – *Bodhisattva* in Mahayana Buddhism. Such bearers of the wisdom tradition have become the object of much admiration within their own religious family but, in some instances, have become world figures as the status of the present Dalai Lama clearly demonstrates. Their lives are also seen as exemplary and, as a consequence, they become models of the ideals of their religious teaching. Hence, it is necessary to somehow think of the sage as an analogous figure to the saint both within and beyond the Christian tradition.

The term "guru" has become so common in modern parlance that it is frequently used as a term to describe anyone who can give the "last word" on any one of a range of skills. Thus we speak of computer gurus or sports gurus, and so on. In Hinduism, however, the *guru* (Sanskrit word for teacher or elder) is one who can initiate a beginner on a spiritual path leading to enlightenment. In Hinduism, some gurus have encapsulated in their persons such spiritual power that their very presence bestows spiritual blessing; they exude *darshan* (power) by their presence. As a teacher of spiritual wisdom, however, the guru bears a certain resemblance to the elder or spiritual master/mistress in the Christian monastic tradition.

At times, the bearer of a wisdom tradition also takes on prophetic functions in the deep sense of the prophet (Greek: *pro + phetes*) as speaking with authority under the name of some transcendental power which, in the biblical tradition, means God. The prophet speaks not with his or her authority nor from power resulting from an office, but with a sense of divine authority. In the twentieth century, the most exemplary figure within this tradition was the late Reverend Martin Luther King, Jr (1929–1968) who preached pacific non-resistance to civil discrimination in the United States of America. King, of course, was deeply in debt to the thought and practice of Mohandas Gandhi, who used non-violent action both in South Africa and India as an instrument of human liberation. King himself identified his mission of speaking about civil rights as one modeled on the great eighth-century prophets of the Old Testament, knowing, like them, that his unpalatable message might well result in his own death. The iconic uses to which King's persona has been put among African Americans (or, similarly, Steve Biko and Nelson Mandela in South Africa) bear more than a slight resemblance to the emblematic power of saintly figures in traditional Catholicism.

There is something almost symbiotic about the modern development of this prophetic witness. Gandhi wedded his own profound experience as a Hindu to the knowledge of the beatitudes of Jesus learned from Tolstoyan pacifists while a law student in England. He took that knowledge home with him, first to South Africa and later to India, to develop his philosophy of non-violence. King learned from Gandhi and used his theory of non-violent peaceful resistance in the American South. His experiences, in turn, were later replicated in civil-rights struggles in places as distant as South Africa and Eastern Europe. In that sense, at least, there was a kind of global awareness of the sanctity of peacemaking and human rights ethics that resulted from a blending of both Indian and biblical insights as they were lived out by different persons of different religious persuasions – persons who often receive the adjective of "saintly."

Finally, in some religious traditions the keepers of the wisdom tradition of a given religious faith are seen not as intercessors or repositories of sacred power or bearers of a prophetic message but as the exemplification of wisdom; they are known simply as the sages. Perhaps the most consistent religious tradition that puts the sage at center stage is Confucianism. Named from its founder Confucius (551–479 BCE), and assimilating the teachings of Mencius (372–289), this Chinese religion honors both men as paradigms of wisdom and their writings as the source for the ethical teachings that are seen as the highest wisdom. The teachings of both men, with their respective emphasis on correct relationships, living in harmony, and humane love (Chinese: *jen*), would not only result in human happiness but in a well-ordered and benevolent political life. Mencius argued, as a successor to Confucius, that such harmony could only come from living the Way (Chinese: *Tao*) of the four virtues of humanity, righteousness, propriety, and wisdom.

The idea of cultivating a path of wisdom, done in the context of a disciplined life devoted to the search for wisdom, was a concept congenial to ancient Greek philosophy. As Pierre Hadot pointed out in his classic work *Philosophy as a Way of Life*, many of the ancient "schools" of philosophy (Platonic, Pythagorean, and so on) demanded a kind of life commitment to ensure that the search for truth was serious. It is not accidental, as Hadot noted, that certain forms of Christian monasticism (for example, ideas in the monastic rules of the Cappadocian, Saint Basil) saw monasticism as the true philosophical life (*bios philosophikos*). The great monastic figures, in this fashion, could also be regarded as sages.

Finally, we should note that there is a certain overlap between these different ideal types of holy people in the world's religions. In this respect, the story of Saints Barlaam and Josaphat is instructive. A Greek life of these two figures can be traced back into the very early medieval period. According to the story, an Indian king was told that one day his son would become a Christian. Despite all of the king's precautions, a hermit named Barlaam did convert the son, named Josaphat. Josaphat, after a period of kingship as a replacement for his father, retreated into the desert where he met Barlaam once again and lived a life of great holiness. After their deaths their bodies were brought back to India and buried there. This story, widely retold in a variety of languages (in the fifteenth century there were even Icelandic and Swedish versions) is, in fact, a Christianized version of a life of the Buddha which somehow came into Christian hands. The name *Josaphat* seems to be an inferior transliteration of the Persian *Budasif* which, in turn, is a transliteration of the word *Bodhisattva*. Despite this transformation of a version of the life of the Buddha into a fictional pair of saints, they were widely honored throughout the Middle Ages with their lives retold in the influential *Golden Legend* and their names inscribed in the Roman martyrology until modern times on their feast day, November 27.

Saints as a Theological Resource

With the rise of academic or scholastic theology in the Middle Ages there was a tendency to separate the study of the saintly life from the serious study of theology. This turn away from monastic forms of theological reflection to more dialectical and scholastic forms had not always been the case. Lives of the saints were part and parcel of the spiritual formation of serious Christians from the time of antiquity. Today, writings about saints are not generally the subject of serious intellectual inquiry unless the saints are revered as much for their scholarship as for their other "saintly" qualities. We tend to be more edified by Aquinas's writings than by the facts of his personal life. This, of course, was not always the case. Augustine tells us in the *Confessions* (VIII. 6) that he and his set were profoundly moved by reading Athanasius' life of the hermit Antony of the Desert. Athanasius himself thought that the life of Antony would serve as an apologetic argument for Christianity against the pagans. Centuries later, Ignatius of Loyola was put on the path of religious conversion by his leisure reading of the lives of the saints while recuperating from war wounds. In our own day, Edith Stein (Teresa Benedicta of the Holy Cross) tells us that her conversion came by a quite accidental reading of Saint Teresa of Avila's autobiography. When she finished the book, she tells us, she said to herself "This is the truth."

It has only been in more recent times that scholars in the theological sciences have begun to look again at the tradition of saintliness as a serious resource both for the study of social history (the seemingly unpromising mountains of saints legends are now mined as a resource for reconstructing what the French call *mentalités*) and for theology. In the latter case, the reason for this turn to the saintly life can be explained as a result of the rise of narrative theology and the various attempts to heal the rift between "spirituality" and "theology." Some decades ago, the late Swiss theologian Hans Urs Von Balthasar lamented the chasm between theology and spirituality and mounted his own attempt to bridge the gap. In the fifth volume of his massive *Theological Aesthetics*, he laid out a "metaphysics of sainthood" as part of a large retrieval of the saintly life as a constituent of his overall theological project.[3] This direction provided other theologians with the impetus needed to consider the tradition of saintliness as a genuine resource for serious theology.

In a recent work on the phenomenology of Christian spirituality, Kees Waaijman has developed a sophisticated method for the hermeneutical retrieval of saintly lives in order to arrive at a core understanding of Christian practice.[4] In this enterprise he has sought to retrieve the hagiographical tradition in order to use it as a resource for a serious grounding for Christian spirituality. Waaijman, speaking of modern spiritual biographies, sets out the three stages in this process. First, the biography provides us with a profile of the person in question while, typically, hinting at the motifs that shaped the person's life. Secondly, the biography may tell us more sharply about the cultural, religious, and spiritual context within which the person lived. It is in this stage that we can detect both the limitations and the innovations of the saintly life by attending to the spiritual matrix which formed the person. Finally, if these first two tasks are done with care, we might be able to get closer to the interior dynamics of the saint's life of faith as "something" beyond the constraints of cultural analysis. To describe only the person in relation to culture is something any perceptive historian should be able to do; to describe the life of grace and response to it is the further step which is precisely theological.

The field of religious studies more generally has interested itself in the ways in which we can speak of "saints" in the various religious traditions of the world, but this has been done mainly at the first two levels described by Waaijman. We have already alluded to the fact that such studies run across problems of terminology. One small example of the difficulty can be gleaned from the fact that at the end of the entry on "holy persons" in the *HarperCollins Dictionary of Religion* (1995) there are reference links to nearly one hundred and thirty-two other topics.[5] Admittedly, some of these are too broad to be useful (for example, acolyte), but others do name categories of holy persons in the various religions of the world. Does, for example, the shaman in tribal religion function analogically to the saint in the major world religions? One could multiply such questions but a careful reading does permit us to spot some similarities without the risk of being overly reductionistic. One of the great tasks facing the theologian today is to inquire whether or not it is productive to move to the third stage and ask theological questions. Such an inquiry is one that has been set by the rise of interest in comparative theology. Such research has become a natural and necessary consequence for Catholic theologians deriving from the positive notions expressed by the Second Vatican Council's Declaration on the Church's Relation to Non-Christian Religions (*Nostra Aetate*).

Finally, we should note that Pope John Paul II, with his keen interest in the saints of the Christian tradition, has incorporated in his own thinking a kind of "theology of the saints." In his Apostolic Letter (*Novo Millenio Ineunte*, 2001) at the end of the Jubilee celebrations for the year 2000 the pope described the "lived theology of the saints" who offer us deep insights that allow us to understand more easily the intuitions of faith. As if to give concrete evidence of that possibility, he interweaves observations from the lives and writings of the saints (Augustine, Benedict, Paulinus of Nola, Teresa of Avila, John of the Cross, Catherine of Siena) throughout his text.

Saints and the Continuity of Religious Tradition

We have noted earlier in this work that in the period of the Catholic Reformation the canonization of saints was used, at least in part, as an apologetic argument for the continued holiness of the Catholic Church and as an implied polemic argued against the churches of the Reformation. The empirical fact of the canon of saints was seen as an argument for the spiritual resources still available within the old Catholic Church. Indeed, before and well into the Baroque period one could say that, while academic theology was not conspicuous for its brilliance, there was a flourishing of spiritualities which were frequently identified with saintly figures: Saints John of the Cross and Teresa of Avila, Saint Francis de Sales, Saint Ignatius of Loyola, the French School, and so on. Closer to our own day (as we have also noted) Pope John Paul II has used the canonization process with some prodigality to hold up the perennial presence of holiness in the church, although he has done so less for polemical purposes and more for purposes of evangelization.

We might well reflect a little further on the role of the saint as a "test" for the vigor of the perennial value of conspicuous saintliness at a time when conventional allegiance to the church is on the wane in many places in the Western world. Is it possible to learn something from those who, borrowing from a formulation made by the late Iris Murdoch in her Gifford Lectures, "throw away" everything out of love for God, Good, and others?[6]

A few years ago, the British theologian Frances Young drew a provocative analogy between Christian practice and music.[7] Let the Bible stand as the primary text. It is studied as a text much in the same way as a musical score is studied by a musicologist, i.e. to establish the authenticity of the text and its most fundamental meaning. However, a musical score is meant to be performed; it is in the performance that the deepest meaning of the score is revealed. That meaning derives both from fidelity to the text and as the score is enhanced by the performance of the musician. Young offers an analogy with the biblical text; namely, that its truest meaning derives from its enactment in performing the Christian life. In both cases, the enactment or performance occurs at various levels of competence. It is one thing for a tyro at the piano to bang out Mozart's *Eine kleine Nachtmusik* and it is quite another thing to hear the same piece being interpreted by a concert-quality performer. Similarly, there are those who give a passing nod to the demands of the gospel life, but it is quite something else when someone grasps the same message and performs at a profound level. The most common fashion in which the Scriptures are "performed" is in the liturgy, in preaching, and in meditation. At times, an individual becomes so grasped by and master of the repertoire that is the Bible that such a person performs at the level of virtuosity.

Let the virtuoso in this analogy stand for the saint. The saint is a "classic" performer of the Word of God. A further point needs to be made: a virtuoso performance of the Christian life does not exist outside the boundaries of history and culture. The "style" of sanctity is made specific by the time and place in which a person finds him or herself. At a certain level this observation is a banality. Only the naïve would think that wearing a brown habit with a hood and a rope girdle constitutes the conditions for Franciscan holiness. Francis took on the clothing of the "little people" (the *minores*) at a time when clothing was a social marker in a way that is not true today. A person wearing a brown robe and sandals today says, by such clothing, "I am religious" not "I am poor."

Now it is true that certain saintly gestures have a perennial validity. Setting aside the obvious benefits of modern airline travel, fax machines, and so on, it is not clear that the work Mother

Teresa of Calcutta did for the poor would be any different had she lived five hundred years ago. Rooted in very traditional Catholic piety, supremely orthodox in matters doctrinal and moral, she saw her life as being of complete service to the poorest and most neglected people. In that sense, Mother Teresa gave witness to the perennial values of Christian charity. She did this at such an intense level that she drew admirers from around the world to collaborate in her work which led in the end to her receiving the Nobel Prize.

Mother Teresa of Calcutta represents a very traditional form of saintliness.[8] The question is, however, whether or not this kind of traditional form of sainthood exhausts the character of saintliness or whether, as many believe, new forms of saintliness are required by the age. This question has been raised most pointedly by those who have been associated with liberation theology. This form of theology, born in the early 1970s in Latin and Central America, raised a very important question: is it sufficient to extend charity, no matter how prodigally, if the conditions that generate poverty are not examined and overcome? Such theologians made it their task to do a careful analysis of societal issues and to confront unjust powers in a prophetic fashion. This direct confrontation of unjust power resulted in an odd, almost singular, situation: political authority, many times invoking patriotism, anti-Marxism, and a political sense of "Christendom," unleashed a lethal attack on their fellow Christians, resulting in the deaths of many bishops, priests, religious sisters, and lay people who espoused liberation for the poor. Such was the fate of the late Archbishop Oscar Romero who was murdered by the Salvadoran military while he was saying mass. Shortly after his death his tomb became a focal point for candles, flowers, and pilgrimages. He has often been compared to Thomas Becket and the Polish Saint Stanislaus as one who was murdered by his own civil authority. Those close to him know that the ordinary people of his country venerate him as a (not yet canonized) saint, but wish to press further to understand a person who overcame his own conservative instincts to commit himself to radical principles in order to arrive at a point where he could say that, if they killed him for those principles, he would "rise again in the people of El Salvador."[9]

Martyrs like Romero and others have clearly understood that allegiance to the faith in places where this allegiance could mean their death at the hands of the political powers entailed a different kind of martyrdom and a different kind of Christian witness. Such persons were living in a kind of postmodern world in which the lingering echoes of the old Christian order were only present in shadowy and vague forms of sentimentality.

Commenting on the death of a Sicilian priest who was murdered by the Mafia in the early 1990s because of his struggles against corruption in the city of Palermo, an Italian theologian, Bartolomeo Sorge made an astute observation. In the early days of Christianity people were martyred out of hatred for the Christian faith (*in odium fidei*), whereas in our age people are martyred because certain people cannot stand the compassion, solidarity, and love that some people show for the poor. They hate love (*in odium caritatis*). In the case of the priest, Don Pino Pugliesi, he was murdered at the orders of people who lived in his own parish.[10] Pugliesi knew the danger involved in his crusade against the Mafia. When his murderer was put on trial for the crime, he said that when he stepped out of the shadows of the priest's apartment, Don Pino looked at him, smiled, and said "I was expecting you."

Each year Christians die violent deaths both in countries that are nominally Christian and in areas which are antagonistic to the West in general and Christianity in particular. Those martyrs may give us a clue to a larger question: namely, what would a truly postmodern saint look like? To be sure, there will be "traditional" saints who are held up for veneration in the manner described in these pages. Both Roman Catholic and Orthodox processes of canonization go on as before. Is there, however, any way to think of what a "new" kind of saint might look like?

The issue of a new kind of saint in the light of the postmodern experience has been raised in a provocative book by Edith Wyschogrod. As she tells us in the opening pages of her dense study, her book makes no pretense of returning to premodern hagiography but seeks a "postmodern expression of excessive desire, a desire on behalf of the Other, that seeks the cessation of another's suffering and the birth of another's joy."[11] What she does find compelling about the tradition of hagiography is that it reflects some typical postmodern concerns: narrativity, corporeality, textuality, and historicality. In other words, we know the saints from their stories; the witness that they inscribe through their bodies (for example, in ascetic practices); their reconstruction based on the "lives" that tell us about them; and their roots in a particular time and place.

Who are these saints? Wyschogrod does not think of them as saints in the traditional sense, nor even as framed within a theistic construct. Her notion of sainthood envisions one whose entire adult life is "devoted to the alleviation of sorrow (the psychological suffering) and pain (the physical suffering) that afflicts other persons without distinction of rank or group or, alternatively, that afflicts sentient beings, whatever the cost to the saint in pain or sorrow."[12]

It is clear from her description of the saint that she is not talking about a person who is a conduit of transcendent power or a bearer of wisdom or an intercessor. Only to the degree that such a person inspires others does this kind of saint stand as a model or exemplar. What Wyschogrod has in mind, it strikes her readers, are those persons who have been tested in the extremities of contemporary experience. What one intuits right away is the person who has stood the test of the death camps, the gulags, the police cellars, the modern deserts of ruined cities, and the holders of integrity under the extremes of war and violence. Since she explicitly allows for fictive persons within her canon, she would probably bring under the penumbra of postmodern sanctity those fictional characters we discussed earlier in this book as well as those who have survived the demonic fires of modernity.

Why are such persons of significance? Wyschogrod's answer is simple enough: they offer a possible new moral path in an age that so urgently needs one. As she says near the end of her work, there is a need for that kind of saintly boldness and risk "for an effort to develop a new altruism in an age grown cynical and hardened to catastrophe: war, genocide, the threat of world-wide ecological collapse, sporadic and unpredictable eruptions of urban violence, the use of torture, the emergence of new diseases." A postmodern saint, she concludes, "shows the traces of these disasters."[13]

Speaking from a quite different theistic and Christian perspective, Pope John Paul II has made a not dissimilar argument. He, more than any other Christian prelate or theologian in our time, has worked out a complex theology of sanctity in general and martyrdom in particular. He has argued that the martyr is the one who willingly risks life itself as a witness to immutable truth and as a testimony for love and charity. He sees the martyr as a testimony against the horrors of the age and a sign of hope for those who resist the implications of what he has called the "culture of death" so characteristic of contemporary life. The saint is a moral witness.[14]

The intellectual distance between the pope and the philosopher is a big one, but both draw on a common font of saintliness that stretches back to the dawn of Christianity. As complex as that tradition is, there are some persistent threads that allow us to examine the tradition and draw, like the good householder of the Gospel, both old things and new. Those whom we know as saints are merely a sample of all who live before the face of God. Countless millions have reached up in an attempt to live the gospel life and, in the words of John Henry Newman, "in process of time, after death, their excellence perhaps gets abroad; and then they become a witness, a specimen of what the Gospel can do and a sample and a pledge of all those other high creations of God, His saints in full number, who die and are never known."[15]

Until they were brutally murdered by a terrorist group in Algeria associated with *al-Qaeda*, seven Trappist monks were among those saintly figures who are never known except by God. Let them stand as saints for our contemporary age as they brushed up against some of the evil forces abroad in the land. Quietly contemplative in nature, the monastery of Tibhirine housed a small community of monks who prayed and worked the land with never an attempt to try to convert their Muslim neighbors. In fact, they provided a prayer room for the local villagers. One of their number, Brother Luc, was a trained physician who ministered without charge to the sick and the elderly. Some of the monks had been in Algeria before as French soldiers but now returned to lead a rustic life of monastic silence.

The monks had been warned to leave their home because of widespread violence in the country with much of it directed towards foreigners in general and the Catholic religious in particular. The community resisted that advice both because they felt a sense of solidarity with the local people and because of their conviction that they could act as silent witnesses to non-violence and peace. Those convictions came to an end in 1996 when an armed group kidnaped seven members of the community and later beheaded them. Only their severed heads were ever recovered.

The story, extraordinary in its own right, became all the more poignant when it was discovered that one of the monks, the prior of the community, Brother Christian, who had studied Islamics in Rome and spearheaded a small group of Christians and Muslims interested in inter-religious dialogue, had earlier written a letter to be opened only in the event of his death. The letter was written to express his own faith, his love for the Algerian people, and his plea that Muslims should not be stereotyped (a problem endemic in French culture because of the large number of North African immigrants in France from former

French colonies); most strikingly, the letter, as it concludes, addresses his murderer: "Yes, for you, too, I wish this thank-you, this 'A Dieu' whose image is in you also, that we may meet in heaven, like good thieves, if it pleases God, our common Father. Amen! Insh'Allah!"[16]

The martyrdom of the Trappists of Algeria contains within its story many of the elements of martyrdom in our day: the intersection of competing cultures; the silent witness of Christians as a minority presence in an alien culture; the willingness to risk all in the name of love; the spirit of dialogue across religious traditions and alien cultures. On reflection, however, one is also struck that such characteristics were also present in the beginnings of Christianity. The lesson there, of course, is that Christianity must always reinvent itself and that reinvention is best carried out when it goes back to its deepest roots, namely, the following of the One who witnessed unto death on a Roman cross only to be proclaimed as the One who overcame death through life.

And so, in many churches today, the ancient and not so ancient saints are frozen in stained-glass windows and parishioners still meet in church basements under the patronage of the Saint Vincent de Paul Society and babies are baptized with the names of patron saints and the liturgy still commemorates the Blessed Mother, John the Baptist, and the apostles, together with the other saints, and the stories of the saints are told in catechism classes and patronal feast days are celebrated each year with more or less pomp. Those are the ways in which the saints are still with us.

Yet, there are others whom we do not invoke by name or memorialize in the arts. They are the many who live quiet lives of unstinting service, who suffer at the hands of hostile regimes, who risk their lives to comfort the afflicted, who love not an abstract humanity but this or that sufferer of AIDS or mentally handicapped child or the street person sprawled in a doorway. Some of them may come to our attention but most will not.

Those who do emerge from anonymity may be canonized but that very process may lead us to think that that is what a saint is. Such a conclusion would be very wrong. The saint may be as close as our nextdoor neighbor or as far away as those places that we have never heard of. What makes them all saints is their capacity to do the ordinary in an extraordinary fashion.

Appendix I: Patron Saints

The custom of designating a particular saint as a "patron" evolved out of the practice of building churches or shrines over the tombs of saintly figures. The earliest record we have of a formal dedication of a church goes back to the early fourth century. Between the seventh and thirteenth centuries, liturgical rites developed for the dedication and/or consecration of a church destined for sacred use. It is noteworthy that the formal dedication of churches involved placing the relics of saints under the altar stone at the time of the church's dedication. In the course of time the saint or saints associated with a particular village, town, or city became known as the patronal saints of those places. To this day, in Rome, the feast of Saints Peter and Paul are celebrated on June 29 as the patronal day of the city. In many places, the patronal feasts of the city (or country) are also public holidays.

The notion of putting a particular place (church or monastery or town) under the patronage of a given saint or saints extended to groups (like craft guilds or confraternities) in such a manner that the idea of a saint as patron received widespread expansion. It is, to this day, a custom for a young person to choose a saint as his or her special patron at the time of confirmation. It has also been a long-standing custom of popes to designate a particular saint as a special patron of a given group of people.

The list of patronal saints is very long indeed. The new edition of John Delaney's *Dictionary of Saints* (2003) lists just under three hundred patrons and another one hundred who are patrons of a given country. Some patrons make eminent sense, such as Saint Joseph, the patron saint of carpenters, or Saints Cosmas and Damien as patrons of physicians since they themselves were doctors. Others are rather tendentious, such as making Saint Januarius (in Italian: Gennaro) patron of blood banks on the grounds that his blood liquefies each year on his feast day in the city of Naples or Saint Thérèse of Lisieux who is patroness of florists because she is said to have promised a shower of roses from heaven after her death. Still others are based on somewhat dubious etymologies like Saint Lucy (Lucia = *lux*, light) who is patroness of those who have eye diseases.

Some of the more famous patron saints include the following:

actors Saint Genesius (martyr in the period of Diocletian who was a converted actor)

air travelers Saint Joseph of Cupertino (a friar who is alleged to have levitated while in ecstasy)

animals Saint Francis of Assisi

book keepers Saint Matthew the Evangelist (the converted tax collector of the Gospel)

brides Saint Nicholas of Myra (famous for his gifts of dowries to poor girls)

cab drivers Saint Fiacre (the first coaches of Paris were to be found hear his hospice)

cooks Saint Martha (the Gospel figure who served Jesus in her home)

dentists Saint Apollonia (her teeth were wrenched out as part of her torture as a martyr)

funeral directors Nicodemus (Gospel figure who donated the tomb for Jesus)

goldsmiths Saint Dunstan (English saint who plied that trade)

hairdressers Saint Martin de Porres (Latin American saint who was a barber)

homeless Saint Benedict Labre (French ascetic who lived homeless in Rome)

lawyers Saint Thomas More (English lawyer and Lord Chancellor in the time of Henry VIII)

married women Saint Monica (mother of Saint Augustine)

monks Saint Benedict of Nursia

mystics Saint John of the Cross

orators Saint John Chrysostom (Chrysostom means "golden tongued")

painters Saint Luke the Evangelist (based on the legend that he painted portraits of the Virgin Mary)

policemen Michael the Archangel (one of the guardian angels)

retreats Saint Ignatius of Loyola (he began the custom for those making his *Spiritual Exercises*)

sailors (among others) Saint Brendan the navigator

shoemakers Saints Crispin and Crispinian (based on their occupation according to an unreliable legend about these third-century martyrs)

sick Saints John of God and Camillus (both founders of orders promoting hospitals)

soldiers Saints George, Joan of Arc, Martin of Tours, Ignatius of Loyola, Sebastian (because of their connections to the military life)

thieves Dismas (the "good" thief crucified next to Christ)

workers Saint Joseph, spouse of the Virgin

writers Saint Francis de Sales (in his day, a noted author)

Appendix II: Iconography of the Saints

Christian iconography refers to the pictorial or symbolic representation of persons, doctrines, stories, or events in the visual arts. It is a highly complex subject since there is a tradition of Christian art that goes back to the age of the martyrs but which over the ages evolved into a complex phenomenon which can be "read" if one understands the conceptual scheme that lies beyond the symbolism. We know, for instance, that the great medieval cathedrals like Chartres had a unifying iconography behind their vast schemes of sculpture and stained glass. Similarly, in the age of the Baroque, artists frequently worked out a total picture (called a *concetto*) to unify architecture, painting, and sculpture. In the Renaissance (especially but not exclusively in the North), artists would often use "hidden" symbolism that referred to Christian ideas or themes; thus, for example, flowers might have a symbolic significance, as could architectural elements or even colors.

Symbols also played an important part in artistic tableaux in which it was necessary for the artist to distinguish who the persons depicted were. The most common symbol, dating back to the time of the late antique Byzantine mosaics, was the use of the nimbus (halo). For a holy person like the Virgin or a saint, the halo was circular (frequently a cross was in the nimbus if it was the person of Christ), while living persons (like a pope or hierarch) were crowned with a square nimbus or the nimbus was omitted. Sometimes God the Father was crowned with a triangular nimbus symbolizing the Trinitarian character of God.

As the cult of the saints became more pronounced, iconographical symbols became attached to the depiction of a given saint to identify that person. In the catacombs, typically, the gravestone of a martyr was simply designated with the letter "M" (for martyr) to which, at times, a crude palm branch was engraved. In the post-Constantinian period, mosaics (and later, painted icons) would typically have the name of the person depicted written on the work itself. At times, the dress or physiognomy of the person would give some indication of who was depicted. Thus, for example, the ascetic Saint Mary of Egypt always appeared as an emaciated woman covered either in rags or by her own disheveled hair, or a converted soldier saint (Theodore or George or Demetrius) would appear in military garb, while a hierarch would be dressed in liturgical vestments or monastic habits but with their names inscribed.

In the West, however, there developed a much more complex iconographical vocabulary. Those symbols, most often identifying markers of the person depicted, could come from various sources. Biblical allusions were most common. Artistic representations of Saints Peter and Paul, for instance, were distinguishable because Paul most often carried a sword ("The Word of God is a two-edged sword"), while Peter holds keys in his hand based on the promise that Jesus made that Peter would have the "keys to the kingdom." The four evangelists were distinguished by the figures "resembling living creatures" described by the prophet Ezekiel (1: 5 ff) which the early church interpreted as types for the Gospel writers: Matthew (winged young man), Mark (lion), Luke (ox), and John (eagle).

Martyred saints most often were depicted with the instruments of their torture or the result of their painful deaths. Often these instruments or body parts reflected stories told of them in the legends which were commonly known in the religious culture of the time. Some of the more sanguinary of such symbols included Saint Agatha, often depicted with a dish containing her severed breasts, or Saint Lucy carrying her eyeballs on a plate or Saint Apollonia holding a set of pincers with a tooth to indicate one of the tortures she underwent. Saint Roch (in Italy: Rocco) is often pictured pointing to plague wounds on his leg. Other saints often are identified by the instruments of their passion: Saint Catherine with her wheel; Saint Lawrence with a metal grill; Saint Barbara with the tower in which it is said she was shut up, and so on. Iconic symbols have such a tenacious hold on the tradition that they not infrequently are found, for example, in stained glass, in churches built in the nineteenth and twentieth centuries, even if, today, viewers are less familiar with the traditional stories of the saints.

At times, saints, especially when they are well known only in a particular geographical area, have scenes in their portrait depicting miraculous incidents related in their legend. The rather obscure eighth-century monk Saint Bertulf, venerated in Flanders, is often shown with an eagle bearing outstretched wings because, according to his legend, the eagle used its wings to protect the saint during heavy rain. The sixth-century French Saint Vedast (in English: Foster) is usually portrayed with a fox with a goose in its mouth because the saint rescued the goose, according to his legend, to restore it to a poor family. Sometimes even a well-known saint like Saint Benedict of Nursia will be shown performing a miracle recounted in Gregory the Great's life of the saint. Without a knowledge of Gregory's stories the iconography becomes opaque. Not to know the story is to miss the significance of the symbol represented.

The close connection of legend and iconography indicates that what is opaque to the contemporary viewer was well known to an early spectator simply because the lives of the saints were so well known. Panel paintings, like the famous Berlingheri altarpiece of Saint Francis, typically have a series of scenes from the early lives of the saint running like a cartoon strip at the edges of the panel, some of which are easily identifiable (for example, Francis preaching to the birds). Such illustrations of incidents are also found in the Christian East both in icons and frescos.

It is interesting to see how artists handle the iconography of modern saints who have been recently beatified or canonized. Those who have died for the faith in the twentieth century, for example, did not lose their lives in the ways described in *The Golden Legend*. A Saint Sebastian may well have been shot to death with arrows but today we see images of modern saints who wear the striped pajamas of the Nazi concentration camp with a background of barbed wire (for example, for Maximilian Kolbe), and allusions are made to bullets and guns. What we see, in short, is the slow evolution of a new iconography suitable for the times in which the modern saints have lived. The very fact of this new iconography is a fair indication that the tradition of iconography is a living rather than a static reality in the Christian tradition.

The scholarship on Christian iconography is voluminous. (George Kaftal's study of iconography in Italian painting up to the fifteenth century alone runs to five large volumes.) The *Dictionary of Christian Art*, edited by Diane Apostolos-Cappadona (1994) is a concise work with a good bibliography of further, more technical studies. The *Biblioteca Sanctorum* (see the Select Bibliography) has a section on iconography for each saint described. The most useful work for iconography in the Eastern Christian tradition is Henry Maguire's *The Icons of their Bodies: Saints and their Images in Byzantium* (1996).

Notes

Chapter 1 The Saint: Beginnings

1   *Butler's Lives of the Saints*, edited by Paul Burns, 12 vols (Collegeville, MN: Liturgical Press, 1995–2000).
2   *Martyrologium Romanum: Editio Typica* (Vatican City: Vatican City Press, 2001) is the most recent edition.
3   In citing conciliar documents in this book, I use *Decrees of the Ecumenical Councils*, edited by Norman Tanner, 2 vols (Washington, DC: Georgetown University Press, 1990).
4   The literature on martyrdom is enormous. I still find reliable W. H. C. Frend's *Martyrdom and Persecution in the Early Church* (Oxford: Oxford University Press, 1965), even though some of his judgments have been modified.
5   The standard collection is *The Acts of the Christian Martyrs*, ed. H. Musurillo, SJ (Oxford: Clarendon Press, 1972; 2nd edn, 1979). For a list of all the Acts and their critical editions, see Hans R. Seeliger, "Acts of the Martyrs," in *Dictionary of Early Christian Literature*, ed. Siegma Dopp et al. (New York: Crossroad, 2000), pp. 405–12.
6   The general reader may find both texts conveniently in the Penguin *Early Christian Writings: The Apostolic Fathers*, ed. Andrew Louth, rev. edn (Harmondsworth: Penguin, 1987).

7   On the development of such calendars, see Kevin Donovan, "The Sanctoral," in *The Study of the Liturgy*, edited by Cheslyn Jones et al. (London: SPCK, 1992), pp. 472–85.

8   On the elaboration of such architectural settings, see John Crook, *The Architectural Setting of the Cult of the Saints in the Early Christian West 300–1200* (Oxford: Oxford University Press, 2000).

9   A good study is Edward Malone, *The Monk and the Martyr* (Washington, DC: Catholic University Press, 1950).

10 A bibliography of the writings of Brown and critical essays on his work may be found in *The Cult of Saints in Late Antiquity and the Middle Ages: Essays on the Contribution of Peter Brown*, edited by James Howard-Johnston and Paul Anthony Hayward (Oxford: Oxford University Press, 1999).

11 These are fully described in Patricia Cox's *Biography in Late Antiquity: A Quest for the Holy Man* (Berkeley, CA: University of California Press, 1983).

12 Clare Stancliffe, *St Martin and his Hagiographer: History and Miracle in Sulpicius Severus*. Oxford Historical Monographs (Oxford: Clarendon Press, 1983).

13 *Life and Miracles of St Benedict* (*Book Two of the Dialogues*), trans. Odo Zimmerman et al. (Collegeville, MN: Liturgical Press, n.d.), p. 77. Gregory notes that Benedict's body was buried in a chapel over what was once an altar to Apollo, thus, implicitly, indicating the power of the saints over pagan deities.

14 See the discussion in Lisa Bitel, *Isle of the Saints: Monastic Settlement and Christian Community in Early Ireland* (Ithaca, NY: Cornell University Press, 1990), pp. 229–34.

Chapter 2 The Bureaucratization of Sanctity

1   The long transformation of Saint Nicholas into Santa Claus is the subject of the book of C. W. Jones, *Saint Nicholas of Myra, Bari, and Manhattan: Biography of a Legend* (Chicago: University of Chicago Press, 1978).

2   Jacobus de Voragine, *The Golden Legend: Readings on the Saints*, trans. William Granger Ryan, 2 vols (Princeton, NJ: Princeton University Press, 1993).

3   The classic study of such pious thefts is Patrick Geary's *Furta Sacra: Thefts of Relics in the Central Middle Ages* (Princeton, NJ: Princeton University Press, 1978).

4   Lisa Bitel's *Isle of the Saints: Monastic Settlement and Christian Community in Early Ireland* (Ithaca, NY: Cornell University Press, 1990) studies this arrangement in detail.

5   The classic study is John Baldovin, SJ, *The Urban Character of Christian Worship: The Origins, Development, and Meaning of the Stational Liturgy* (Rome: Pontifical Institute of Oriental Studies, 1987).

6   Jacques Delarun's *The Misadventure of Francis of Assisi* (St Bonaventure, NY: Franciscan Institute, 2002) is a reliable guide to the vexatious issue of the polemical use of the various legends.

7   I base my information on *The Byzantine Saint*, ed. Sergei Hakel (London: Fellowship of St Alban and St Sergius, 1981) with special attention to the essay of Ruth Macrides, "Saints and Sainthood in the Early Palaiologian Period," pp. 67–87.

8   On this tradition, see John Saward, *Perfect Fools: Folly for Christ's Sake in Catholic and Orthodox Spirituality* (Oxford: Oxford University Press, 1980).

9   See Mary Lee Nolan and Sidney Nolan, *Christian Pilgrimage in Modern Western Europe* (Chapel Hill, NC: University of North Carolina Press, 1989) for historical background.

10 These treatises are newly translated: *Three Treatises on the Divine Images: Saint John of Damascus*, trans. Andrew Louth (Crestwood, NY: St Vladimir's Seminary Press, 2003).

Chapter 3 Reformations: Protestant and Catholic

1   Introduction to *Devotio Moderna: Basic Writings*, ed. John Van Engen (New York: Paulist Press, 1988), p. 27.

2   Eamon Duffy, *The Stripping of the Altars: Popular Religion in England 1400–1580* (New Haven, CT: Yale University Press, 1992).

3   The full text is in *Creeds and Confessions of Faith in the Christian Tradition*, vol. 2, edited by Jaroslav Pelikán and Valerie Hotchkiss (New Haven, CT: Yale University Press, 2003), p. 466. Such examples could be multiplied.

4   Ibid., vol. 2, p. 873.

5 Donald Weinstein and Rudolph M. Bell, *Saints and Society: The Two Worlds of Western Christendom 1000–1700* (Chicago: University of Chicago Press, 1982) is an excellent survey of the evidence.

6 The Rules are part of the *Spiritual Exercises*. See *The Spiritual Exercises of Saint Ignatius of Loyola*, edited by George E. Ganss, SJ (New York: Paulist Press, 1991), pp. 211–14 for the complete text.

7 For a brilliant account of martyrdom in this period, see Brad S. Gregory, *Salvation at Stake: Christian Martyrdom in Early Modern Europe* (Cambridge, MA: Harvard University Press, 1999).

8 Carla Gardina Pastrana, "Martyred by the Saints: Quaker Executions in Seventeenth Century Massachusetts," in *Colonial Saints: Discovering the Holy in the Americas*, edited by Allan Greer and Jodi Bilinkoff (London: Routledge, 2003), pp. 169–91. This entire volume is an excellent source for a study of the saints in the Americas.

9 For a fuller exposition of the older canonization process, see *Lives of the Saints*, edited by Richard McBrien (San Francisco: Harper, 2001), pp. 41–54.

10 A sophisticated account of the Bollandists may be found in Dom David Knowles's *Great Historical Enterprises* (Cambridge: Cambridge University Press, 1963), pp. 1–32.

Chapter 4 Towards the Modern World

1 In 1940 the Vatican did create a list of feast days for saints from the Christian (largely Russian) East for the benefit of Russian Catholics who were in union with Rome.

2 Their order almost foundered when the third general, Bernardino Ochino, defected to Protestantism in 1541.

3 For a general survey of women's religious life, see Jo Ann McNamara, *Sisters in Arms: Catholic Nuns through Two Millennia* (Cambridge, MA: Harvard University Press, 1996).

4 For a good introduction to the evolution of the category of Doctor of the Church, see Bernard McGinn, *The Doctors of the Church* (New York: Crossroad, 1999). Whether women could actually teach "doctrine" was the subject of heated debate in Rome with the discussion nicely studied in Steven Payne's *Saint Thérèse of Lisieux: Doctor of the Universal Church* (London: St Paul Publications, 2003).

5 See McGinn, *Doctors of the Church* for a representative example.

6 There is an analogy with the Oriental *guru* who serves a somewhat similar function.

7 Sergius Bolshakoff, *Russian Mystics* (Kalamazoo, MI: Cistercian Publications, 1976), pp. 122–44. The same book has an interesting chapter on the elders of Optino Monastery (pp. 164–95).

8 Matthew the Poor, *Orthodox Prayer Life: The Interior Way* (Crestwood, NY: St Vladimir's Seminary Press, 2003).

9 C. Bard Faught's *The Oxford Movement* (University Park, PA: Pennsylvania State University Press, 2003) provides a tidy account of the movement with an ample bibliography.

10 The whole question of Newman and the project of the lives of the saints is discussed in Ian Ker, *John Henry Newman: A Biography* (Oxford: Oxford University Press, 1988), pp. 281ff. Ker points out (pp. 248–9) that Newman was writing on ecclesiastical miracles quite independently of the project on the lives of the saints.

Chapter 5 The Twentieth Century

1 I borrow here from *The French School of Spirituality*, ed. Raymond Deville (Pittsburgh, PA: Duquesne University Press, 1994), p. 153ff.

2 This language is inspired by David Tracy's discussion of the "classic" in *The Analogical Imagination* (New York: Crossroad, 1981).

3 Paul Mariani's *Thirty Days: On Retreat with the Exercises of St Ignatius* (Harmondsworth: Penguin, 2002) is an excellent example, written by a literary critic, of learning the Ignatian way.

4 Karl Rahner, "The Church of the Saints," in *Theological Investigations*, vol. 3 (London: Darton, Longman, and Todd, 1967), pp. 91–105.

5 I have pursued this theme of the saintly outsider in more detail in my book *The Meaning of Saints* (San Francisco: Harper and Row, 1981).

6 Theodore Ziolkowski, *Fictional Transfigurations of Jesus* (Princeton, NJ: Princeton University Press, 1972).

7 E. M. Cioran, *Tears and Saints* (Chicago: University of Chicago Press, 1995), p. 10.

8 Ibid., p. 22.

9   The best survey in English is Robert Royal's *The Catholic Martyrs of the Twentieth Century* (New York: Crossroad, 2000); a more comprehensive work is Andrea Ricciardi's *Il secolo del martirio: I cristiani nel novecento* (Milan: Mondadori, 2000).

10 The literature on martyrdom is enormous. I have surveyed some of it in "On Contemporary Martyrs: Some Recent Literature," *Theological Studies* 63 (2002), pp. 374–81.

11 On the thinking of Pope John Paul II on martyrdom, see my essay "The Universal Call to Holiness: Martyrs of Charity and Witnesses to Truth," in *The New Catholic Encyclopedia Jubilee Volume: The Wojtyla Years* (Washington, DC: The Catholic University of America, 2001), pp. 109–16.

12 They are profiled in Giampolo Mattei, *Ucraina terra di martiri* (Vatican City: L'Osservatore Romano, 2002). Their stories are little known in the West outside ethnic communities.

13 Jon Sobrino, *Witnesses to the Kingdom* (Maryknoll, NY: Orbis, 2003).

14 For profiles of all the martyrs depicted in Westminster Abbey's homage to the contemporary martyrs, see *The Terrible Alternative*, ed. Andrew Chandler (London: Cassell, 1998).

15 The most informative study of the entire process is Kenneth Woodward's *Making Saints* (New York: Simon and Schuster, 1990).

16 See, for example, *The One Mediator, the Saints, and Mary: Lutherans and Catholics in Dialogue*, vol. 8, ed. George Anderson et al. (Minneapolis, MN: Augsburg/Fortress, 1992).

Chapter 6 The Saints, World Religions, and the Future

1   See, for example, these studies: *Saints and Virtues*, ed. John Stratton Hawley (Berkeley, CA: University of California Press, 1987); *Sainthood: Its Manifestations in World Religions*, ed. Richard Kieckhefer and George D. Bond (Berkeley, CA: University of California Press, 1988); *Women Saints in World Religions*, ed. Arvid Sharma (Albany, NY: State University of New York Press, 2000).

2   A parallel list may be found in the New Testament Epistle to the Hebrews (11: 4–38) praising the great Old Testament persons of faith.

3   Hans Urs Von Balthasar, *The Glory of the Lord: A Theological Aesthetics*, vol. 5 (San Francisco, CA: Ignatius, 1991). William Thompson's

Fire and Light: The Saints and Theology (New York: Paulist Press, 1987) was a first attempt to do such a constructive retrieval using the saints as a theological resource. Elizabeth Johnson's *Friends of God and Prophets* (New York: Continuum, 1998) works in the same vein from a feminist perspective.

4   Kees Waaijman, *Spirituality: Forms, Foundations, Methods* (Leuven: Peeters, 2002), pp. 617–21.

5   "Holy Persons" in *HarperCollins Dictionary of Religion*, ed. Jonathan Z. Smith (San Francisco, CA: HarperCollins, 1995), pp. 461–4 at p. 464.

6   Iris Murdoch, *Metaphysics as a Guide to Morals* (Harmondsworth: Penguin, 1992).

7   Frances Young, *The Art of Performance: Towards a Theology of Holy Scripture* (London: Darton, Longman, and Todd, 1990); published in the United States as *Virtuoso Theology* (Cleveland: Pilgrim, 1993).

8   Mother Teresa's formal beatification took place on October 19, 2003 at a ceremony that was to mark the 25th anniversary of John Paul II's papacy.

9   Jon Sobrino's *Archbishop Romero: Memories and Reflections* (Maryknoll, NY: Orbis, 1990) raises the issue of his sanctity with theological acumen.

10 See Francesco Deliziosi, *Don Pugliesi* (Milan: Mondadori, 2001) for a detailed study of the priest's life and death.

11 Edith Wyschogrod, *Saints and Postmodernism: Revisioning Moral Philosophy* (Chicago: University of Chicago Press, 1990), p. xxiv.

12 Ibid., p. 34.

13 Ibid., p. 257.

14 See my "The Universal Call to Holiness: Martyrs of Charity and Witnesses to Truth," in *The New Catholic Encyclopedia Jubilee Volume: The Wojtyla Years* (Washington, DC: The Catholic University of America, 2001), pp. 109–16.

15 John Henry Newman, *Parochial and Plain Sermons* (San Francisco, CA: Ignatius, 1997), p. 832.

16 The text may be found in John Kiser's *The Monks of Tibhirine* (New York: St Martin's Press, 2002), pp. 245–6. I have slightly amended Kiser's translation.

Select Bibliography

Lives of the Saints

Acta Sanctorum (Antwerp, 1643) [Bollandist scholarship].

Biblioteca Sanctorum, 12 vols (Rome: Lateran, 1960–1970) [in Italian with a supplementary volume published in 1987].

Burns, Paul (ed.), *Butler's Lives of the Saints*, 12 vols (Collegeville, MN: Liturgical Press, 1995–2000).

Delaney, John (ed.), *Dictionary of Saints*, rev. edn by Arthur Jones (Garden City, NY: Doubleday, 2003).

Ellsberg, Robert, *All Saints* (New York: Crossroad, 1997) [ecumenical selections for a saint for each day of the calendar year].

Farmer, David H. (ed.), *The Oxford Dictionary of Saints*, 3rd edn (Oxford: Oxford University Press, 1993) [saints of the British Isles; excellent bibliographies].

Jones, Kathleen, *Women Saints* (Tunbridge Wells: Burns and Oates, 1999; Maryknoll, NY: Orbis, 1999).

McBrien, Richard (ed.), *Lives of the Saints* (San Francisco: Harper, 2001) [useful appendices].

Noble, T. and Head, T., *Soldiers of Christ: Saints and Saints' Lives from Late Antiquity and the Early Middle Ages* (University Park, PA: Pennsylvania State University Press, 1995).

Ryan, William Granger (trans.), *Jacobus de Voragine, The Golden Legend: Readings on the Saints* (Princeton, NJ: Princeton University Press, 1993).

Works Cited

Anderson, George et al., *The One Mediator, the Saints, and Mary: Lutherans and Catholics in Dialogue*, vol. 8 (Minneapolis, MN: Augsburg/Fortress, 1992).

Apostolos-Cappadona, Diane (ed.), The *Dictionary of Christian Art* (New York: Continuum, 1994).

Baldovin, John, *The Urban Character of Christian Worship: The Origins, Development, and Meaning of the Stational Liturgy* (Rome: Pontifical Institute of Oriental Studies, 1987).

Bitel, Lisa, *Isle of the Saints: Monastic Settlement and Christian Community in Early Ireland* (Ithaca, NY: Cornell University Press, 1990).

Bolshakoff, Sergius, *Russian Mystics* (Kalamazoo, MI: Cistercian Publications, 1976).

Chandler, Andrew (ed.), *The Terrible Alternative* (London: Cassell, 1998).

Cioran, E. M., *Tears and Saints* (Chicago: University of Chicago Press, 1995).

Cox, Patricia, *Biography in Late Antiquity: A Quest for the Holy Man* (Berkeley, CA: University of California Press, 1983).

Crook, John, *The Architectural Setting of the Cult of the Saints in the Early Christian West 300–1200* (Oxford: Oxford University Press, 2000).

Cunningham, L. S., "On Contemporary Martyrs: Some Recent Literature," *Theological Studies* 63 (2002), pp. 374–81.

—— "A Decade of Research on the Saints," *Theological Studies* 53 (1992), pp. 517–33.

—— *The Meaning of Saints* (San Francisco: Harper and Row, 1981).

—— "Saints and Martyrs: Some Contemporary Considerations," *Theological Studies* 60 (1999), pp. 529–37.

—— "The Universal Call to Holiness: Martyrs of Charity and Witnesses to Truth," in *The New Catholic Encyclopedia Jubilee Volume: The Wojtyla Years* (Washington, DC: The Catholic University of America, 2001), pp. 109–16.

Delarun, Jacques, *The Misadventure of Francis of Assisi* (St Bonaventure, NY: Franciscan Institute, 2002).

Deliziosi, Francesco, *Don Pugliesi* (Milan: Mondadori, 2001).

Deville, Raymond (ed.), *The French School of Spirituality* (Pittsburgh, PA: Duquesne University Press, 1994).

Donovan, Kevin, "The Sanctoral," in *The Study of the Liturgy*, ed. Cheslyn Jones et al. (London: SPCK, 1992), pp. 472–85.

Duffy, Eamon, *The Stripping of the Altars: Popular Religion in England 1400–1580* (New Haven, CT: Yale University Press, 1992).

Faught, C. Bard, *The Oxford Movement* (University Park, PA: Pennsylvania State University Press, 2003).

Frend, W. H. C., *Martyrdom and Persecution in the Early Church* (Oxford: Oxford University Press, 1965).

Ganss, George E. (ed.), *The Spiritual Exercises of Saint Ignatius of Loyola* (New York: Paulist Press, 1991).

Geary, Patrick, *Furta Sacra: Thefts of Relics in the Central Middle Ages* (Princeton, NJ: Princeton University Press, 1978).

Gregory, Brad S., *Salvation at Stake: Christian Martyrdom in Early Modern Europe* (Cambridge, MA: Harvard University Press, 1999).

Hakel, Sergei (ed.), *The Byzantine Saint* (London: Fellowship of St Alban and St Sergius, 1981).

Hawley, John Stratton (ed.), *Saints and Virtues* (Berkeley, CA: University of California Press, 1987).

Howard-Johnston, James and Hayward, Paul Anthony (eds), *The Cult of Saints in Late Antiquity and the Middle Ages: Essays on the Contribution of Peter Brown* (Oxford: Oxford University Press, 1999).

Johnson, Elizabeth, *Friends of God and Prophets* (New York: Continuum, 1998).

Jones, C. W., *St Nicholas of Myra, Bari, and Manhattan: Biography of a Legend* (Chicago: University of Chicago Press, 1978).

Ker, Ian, *John Henry Newman: A Biography* (Oxford: Oxford University Press, 1988).

Kieckhefer, Richard and Bond, George D. (eds), *Sainthood: Its Manifestations in World Religions* (Berkeley, CA: University of California Press, 1988).

Kiser, John, *The Monks of Tibhirine* (New York: St Martin's Press, 2002).

Knowles, David, *Great Historical Enterprises* (Cambridge: Cambridge University Press, 1963).

Louth, Andrew (ed.), *Early Christian Writings: The Apostolic Fathers* (Harmondsworth: Penguin, 1987).

—— (trans.), *Three Treatises on the Divine Images: Saint John of Damascus* (Crestwood, NY: St Vladimir's Seminary Press, 2003).

McGinn, Bernard, *The Doctors of the Church* (New York: Crossroad, 1999).

McNamara, Jo Ann, *Sisters in Arms: Catholic Nuns through Two Millennia* (Cambridge, MA: Harvard University Press, 1996).

Maguire, Henry, *The Icons of their Bodies: Saints and their Images in Byzantium* (Princeton, NJ: Princeton University Press, 1996).

Malone, Edward, *The Monk and the Martyr* (Washington, DC: The Catholic University of America, 1950).

Mariani, Paul, *Thirty Days: On Retreat with the Exercises of St Ignatius* (Harmondsworth: Penguin, 2002).

Martyrologium Romanum: Editio Typica (Vatican City: Vatican City Press, 2001).

Mattei, Giampolo, *Ucraina: terra di martiri* (Vatican City: L'Osservatore Romano, 2002).

Matthew the Poor, *Orthodox Prayer Life: The Interior Way* (Crestwood, NY: St Vladimir's Seminary Press, 2003).

Murdoch, Iris, *Metaphysics as a Guide to Morals* (Harmondsworth: Penguin, 1992).

Musurillo, Herbert (ed.), *The Acts of the Christian Martyrs*, 2nd edn (Oxford: Clarendon Press, 1979).

Newman, John Henry, *Parochial and Plain Sermons* (San Francisco, CA: Ignatius, 1997).

Nolan, Mary Lee and Nolan, Sidney, *Christian Pilgrimage in Modern Western Europe* (Chapel Hill, NC: University of North Carolina Press, 1989).

Pastrana, Carla Gardina, "Martyred by the Saints: Quaker Executions in Seventeenth Century Massachusetts," in *Colonial Saints: Discovering the Holy in the Americas*, ed. Allan Greer and Jodi Bilinkoff (London: Routledge, 2003), pp. 169–91.

Payne, Steven, *Saint Thérèse of Lisieux: Doctor of the Universal Church* (New York: St Paul Publications, 2003).

Pelikán, Jaroslav and Hotchkiss, Valerie (eds), *Creeds and Confessions of Faith in the Christian Tradition*, 4 vols (New Haven, CT: Yale University Press, 2003).

Rahner, Karl, "The Church of the Saints," in *Theological Investigations*, vol. 3 (London: Darton, Longman, and Todd, 1967), pp. 91–105.

Ricciardi, Andrea, *Il secolo del martirio: i cristiani nel novecento* (Milan: Mondadori, 2000).

Royal, Robert, *The Catholic Martyrs of the Twentieth Century* (New York: Crossroad, 2000).

Saward, John, *Perfect Fools: Folly for Christ's Sake in Catholic and Orthodox Spirituality* (Oxford: Oxford University Press, 1980).

Seeliger, Hans R., "Acts of the Martyrs," in *Dictionary of Early Christian Literature*, ed. Siegma Dopp et al. (New York: Crossroad, 2000), pp. 405–12.

Sharma, Arvid (ed.), *Women Saints in World Religions* (Albany, NY: State University of New York Press, 2000).

Smith, Jonathan Z. (ed.), *HarperCollins Dictionary of Religion* (San Francisco: HarperCollins, 1995).

Sobrino, Jon, *Archbishop Romero: Memories and Reflections* (Maryknoll, NY: Orbis, 1990).

—— *Witnesses to the Kingdom* (Maryknoll, NY: Orbis, 2003).

Stancliffe, Clare, *St Martin and is Hagiographer: History and Miracle in Sulpicius Severus* (Oxford: Clarendon Press, 1983).

Tanner, Norman (ed.), *Decrees of the Ecumenical Councils.* 2 vols (Washington, DC: Georgetown University Press, 1990).

Thompson, William, *Fire and Light: The Saints and Theology* (New York: Paulist Press, 1987).

Tracy, David, *The Analogical Imagination* (New York: Crossroad, 1981).

Van Engen, John (ed.), *Devotio Moderna: Basic Writings* (New York: Paulist Press, 1988).

Von Balthasar, Hans Urs, *The Glory of the Lord: A Theological Aesthetics*, vol. 5 (San Francisco, CA: Ignatius, 1987).

Waaijman, Kees, *Spirituality: Forms, Foundations, Methods* (Leuven: Peeters, 2002).

Weinstein, Donald and Bell, Rudolph M., *Saints and Society: The Two Worlds of Western Christendom 1000–1700* (Chicago: University of Chicago Press, 1982).

Wilson, Stephen (ed.), *Saints and their Cults* (Cambridge: Cambridge University Press, 1983).

Woodward, Kenneth, *Making Saints* (New York: Simon and Schuster, 1990).

Wyschogrod, Edith, *Saints and Postmodernism: Revisioning Moral Philosophy* (Chicago: University of Chicago Press, 1990).

Young, Frances, *The Art of Performance: Towards a Theology of Holy Scripture* (London: Darton, Longman, and Todd, 1990) (published in the USA as *Virtuoso Theology* [Cleveland: Pilgrim, 1993]).

Zimmerman, Odo et al. (trans.), *Life and Miracles of St Benedict (Book Two of the Dialogues)* (Collegeville, MN: Liturgical Press, n.d.).

Ziolkowski, Theodore, *Fictional Transfigurations of Jesus* (Princeton, NJ: Princeton University Press, 1972).

Other Works Consulted

Abou-El-Haj, B., *The Medieval Cult of Saints* (London: Cambridge University Press, 1995).

Ashton, Gail, *The Generation of Identity in Late Medieval Hagiography* (London: Routledge, 2000).

Bergman, Susan (ed.), *Martyrs: Contemporary Writers on Modern Lives of Faith* (San Francisco: HarperCollins, 1996).

Boyarin, Daniel, *Dying for God: Martyrdom and the Making of Christianity and Judaism* (Stanford: Stanford University Press, 1999).

Brown, Peter, *The Cult of the Saints* (Berkeley, CA: University of California Press, 1981).

Cross, F. L. (ed.), *The Oxford Dictionary of the Christian Church*, 3rd edn (Oxford: Oxford University Press, 1997).

Dictionnaire de spiritualité (Paris, 1937–).

Dizionario degli istituti di perfezione, 10 vols (Rome: Paoline, 1974–).

Duffy, Eamon, *The Voices of Morebath* (New Haven, CT: Yale University Press, 2001).

Galatariotou, C., *The Making of a Saint: The Life, Times and Sanctification of Neophytus the Recluse* (London: Cambridge University Press, 1991).

Heffernan, Thomas, *Sacred Biography: Saints and their Biographers in the Middle Ages* (Oxford: Oxford University Press, 1988).

Kiekehefer, R., *Unquiet Souls: Fourteenth Century Saints and their Religious Milieu* (Chicago: University of Chicago Press, 1984).

Kleinberg, A., *Prophets in their own Country: Living Saints and the Making of Sainthood in the Later Middle Ages* (Chicago: University of Chicago Press, 1992).

Neville, Robert, *Soldier, Sage, Saint* (Albany, NY: State University of New York Press, 1978).

Sherry, Patrick, *Spirits, Saints, Immortality* (Albany, NY: State University of New York Press, 1984).

Spidlik, Tomas, *The Spirituality of the Christian East* (Kalamazoo, MI: Cistercian Publications, 1986).

Van Dam, R., *Saints and their Miracles in Late Antique Gaul* (Princeton, NJ: Princeton University Press, 1993).

Ward, Benedicta, *Miracles and the Medieval Mind* (Philadelphia, PA: University of Pennsylvania Press, 1982).

Wood, Diana (ed.), *Martyrs and Martyrologies* (Oxford: Blackwell, 1993).

Index